Ornamental Grasses

Mary Hockenberry Meyer

Ornamental Grasses

Decorative Plants For Home and Garden

Charles Scribner's Sons, New York

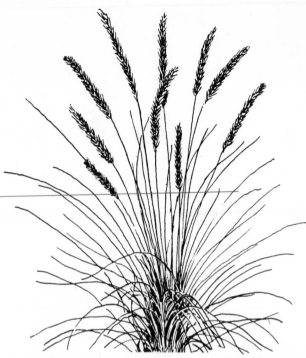

Library of Congress Cataloging in Publication Data
Meyer, Mary Hockenberry.
  Ornamental grasses.
  Includes index.
  1. Ornamental grasses. 2. Ornamental grasses—
Varieties. I. Title.
SB431.7.M48   635.9′34′9   75-11720
  ISBN 0-684-14300-3

The author wishes to thank the following for the line drawings included in this
text: Meryl Meisler, Figure 1; Paul Schueler, Figures 2, 4, 7, 8, 13; Marjery
Koch, Figures 3, 12; and Martha A. Sherwood, Figures 5, 6, 9–11, 14, 15–20.

Contents

Introduction

Horticulturists are constantly faced with the need for suitable plants which will grow and flourish in the man-made landscape in which we live. Tolerance to air pollutants, ability to withstand poor growing conditions plus disease and insect-free species are just a few of the prerequisites for plant materials that now must be used to landscape numerous artificial environments.

Unfortunately, the list of tough, dependable and yet attractive plants for diverse, difficult sites is not only short but very incomplete.

In the search for new plants to fill the demanding locations of the twentieth century a group which has been totally overlooked are grasses—the decorative, ornamental grasses that range in height from 6 inches to 20 feet, in color from silvery-blue to golden-yellow, and survive the winters as far north as central New York.

At least 80 kinds of ornamental grasses are suitable for traditional garden use, in perennial borders, rock gardens, near ponds, streams, etc. Many have decorative flowers which are excellent for dried arrangements.

This book has been written to introduce these grasses to American gardeners. Long popular in Europe, decorative grasses are rarely found in gardens throughout the United States. It is hoped that this book will provide the cultural information necessary for growing the grasses and further stimulate an appreciation for these unique and versatile plants.

Included in this text are several grass-like plants considered and sold in the trade as ornamental grasses, but which are actually members of the Iris, Sedge, or Lily families; the Bamboos are not included.

1.
Where the Ornamental Grasses Originate

Although often tropical in appearance, many of the ornamental grasses are native to cool or mild regions of North America and Europe. This explains why many of the plants are hardy in northern regions of the United States. A few species do originate from tropical or warm climates and thus are difficult to grow in temperate areas.

Over 30 decorative grasses can be found growing wild in the United States and Canada, while Central and South America have at least 9 indigenous species. Forty-eight grasses are native to Great Britain, Europe, and Asia. Approximately 6 species are found in Africa and another 6 in Japan and China.

Festuca spp., *Avena* spp., *Deschampsia* spp., and *Koeleria* spp. are examples of grasses native to North Temperate regions of the world, where cool seasons prevail. Many that are originally native to Europe, such as *Holcus* spp., *Lagurus ovatus*, *Phalaris* spp., *Apera* spp., and *Briza* spp. have been introduced in the United States and are now well-established here.

Cortaderia selloana and *Cymbopogon* spp. are characteristic of South America and found native only in that continent. On the other hand, *Polypogon monspeliensis* can withstand a wide range of climatic conditions, from Europe to North America and southward to Argentina.

Pennisetum spp., *Rhynchelytrum roseum*, *Eragrostis* spp., and *Oplismenus compositus* "Vittatus" are typical indigenous African species. *Miscanthus* spp., *Pennisetum alopecuroides*, and

Carex morrowii "Variegata" are examples of the grasses native to Japan and China.

It is often quite helpful to know the origin of a plant in order to grow it successfully. Dormancy requirements, temperature tolerances, and seasonal variations may be indicated in the nativity of a plant. Interior potted plants, for instance, should be attractive year-round and have no obvious dormant or resting period. Grasses native to tropical or warm climates may have less requirement for a dormant period than those plants from say, Central North America. *Oplismenus compositus* "Vittatus," Basket Grass, for example, can be grown successfully as a house plant, its origin being in Africa. This species probably needs no dormant period. Unfortunately, the dormancy requirement of all the grasses has not yet been determined.

The nativity of a plant can also be a key to important cultural requirements. *Uniola latifolia,* Northern Sea Oats, prefers shady or semi-shady locations rather than full sun. It is indigenous to woodlands and forests in the eastern and southern United States. *Rhynchelytrum roseum,* Ruby Grass, a native of sunny South Africa, is most attractive when grown in full sun; plants in the shade are weaker and have fewer blooms.

Many of the ornamental grasses are cultivars, or natural variations of the species. For example, *Miscanthus sinensis* "Variegatus" is the white striped form of *Miscanthus sinensis* while *Festuca ovina* "Glauca" is the silvery blue form of *Festuca ovina.* The origin of these cultivars is not always known. Most probably they occurred naturally along with the species and are now available due to propagation by nurserymen and interested gardeners.

The origin of specific grasses can be found in the list which follows.

ORIGIN OF ORNAMENTAL GRASSES

BOTANICAL NAME	COMMON NAME	ORIGIN
Acorus gramineus "Variegatus"	Japanese Sweet Flag	Central & East Asia
Agrostis nebulosa	Cloud Grass	Spain
Aira capillaris var. *pulchella*	Hair Grass	Mediterranean region
Alopecurus pratensis "Aureus"	Meadow Foxtail	Eurasia; I*
Ampelodesmos mauritanicus		Mediterranean; I in Southern Cal.
Andropogon scoparius	Little Bluestem	Midwest & Southern U.S.
Apera interrupta	Dense Silky Bent Grass	Europe; I
Apera spica-venti	Loose Silky Bent Grass	Europe; I
Arrhenatherum elatius var. *bulbosum* "Variegatum"	Tall or Bulbous Oat Grass	Europe; I
Arundo donax	Giant Reed	Southern Europe; Asia; I in tropical America
Arundo donax "Versicolor"	Variegated Giant Reed	Southern Europe; Asia; I in tropical America
Avena fatua	Wild Oats	N. America & Europe
Avena sterilis	Animated Oats	N. America & Europe
Bouteloua gracilis	Mosquito Grass; Side Oats Grama	N. America
Briza maxima	Big Quaking Grass	Europe
Briza media	Quaking Grass	Europe; I
Briza minor	Little Quaking Grass	Europe

*I=Introduced in the United States

BOTANICAL NAME	COMMON NAME	ORIGIN
Bromus macrostachys	Brome Grass	Europe, esp Mediterranean region; I
Bromus madritensis	Brome Grass	Europe, esp Mediterranean region; I
Bromus sp.	Brome Grass	Europe, esp Mediterranean region; I
Calamagrostis epigeous	Reed Grass	Europe, Asia; I
Carex buchananii	Leatherleaf Sedge Grass	Europe
Carex morrowii "Variegata"	Japanese Sedge Grass	Japan
Carex pendula	Sedge Grass	Europe
Carex riparia "Variegata"	Pond Sedge	Europe; Britain, Asia
Coix lacryma-jobi	Job's Tears	East Asia, Malaya
Cortaderia selloana & variants	Pampas Grass	South America
Cymbopogon citratus	Lemon Grass	South America
Dactylis glomerata "Variegata"	Variegated Cock's-foot Grass	U.S. & Eurasia
Deschampsia caespitosa & variants	Tufted Hair Grass	Temperate N. America; Europe; Arctic
Deschampsia flexuosa	Wavy Hair Grass	U.S.; Mexico; Eurasia
Desmazeria sicula		Europe
Elymus arenarius	Blue Lyme Grass; Blue Wild Rye	Britain; Europe
Elymus glaucus	Blue Lyme Grass;	Western Canada; U.S.
Elymus interruptus	Nodding Lyme Grass	Midwestern U.S.

BOTANICAL NAME	COMMON NAME	ORIGIN
Eragrostis abyssinica	Love Grass	Africa
Eragrostis curvula	Weeping Love Grass	Africa; I in Midwest
Eragrostis trichodes	Sand Love Grass	Midwestern U.S.
Erianthus ravennae	Plume Grass or Ravennae Grass	Europe, esp. Italy
Festuca amethystina	Large Blue Fescue	Europe
Festuca gigantea	Giant Fescue	Europe; I
Festuca ovina "Glauca" & variants	Blue Fescue	Temperate N. America; Eurasia
Festuca ovina var. *duriuscula*	Hard Fescue	Europe; I
Glyceria maxima "Variegata"	Sweet or Manna Grass	Europe; Temperate Asia; I
Helictotrichon sempervirens	Blue Oat Grass	Europe
Holcus lanatus "Variegatus"	Velvet Grass	Europe; I
Holcus mollis "Variegatus"	Velvet Grass	Europe; I
Hordeum jubatum	Squirrel's-tail Grass	N. America; Eurasia
Hordeum vulgare	Barley	Cultivation
Hystrix patula	Bottlebrush Grass	Eastern U.S.
Imperata sp.	Satintail	Southern & Western U.S.; Mexico
Koeleria cristata "Glauca"	June Grass	Temperate N. America; Eurasia
Lagurus ovatus	Hare's-tail Grass	Mediterranean; I
Lamarkia aurea	Golden Top	Mediterranean; I
Luzula spp.	White Woodrush	Europe
Melica altissima "Atropurpurea"	Melic Grass	Eurasia
Millium effusum "Aureum"	Millet Grass	Eurasia; N. America; Canada

BOTANICAL NAME	COMMON NAME	ORIGIN
Miscanthus sacchariflorus	Eulalia Grass	Asia
Miscanthus sacchariflorus "Giganteus"	Giant Eulalia	Asia
Miscanthus sinensis	Eulalia Grass	Japan & China
Miscanthus sinensis "Gracillimus"	Maiden Grass	Japan & China
Miscanthus sinensis "Variegatus"	Striped Eulalia	Japan & China
Miscanthus sinensis "Zebrinus"	Zebra Grass	Japan & China
Molinea caerulea "Variegata"	Purple Moor Grass	Eurasia; I
Oplismenus compositus "Vittatus"	Basket Grass	Tropical Africa; America
Panicum virgatum & Variants	Switch Grass	N. & Central America
Pennisetum alopecuroides	Fountain Grass	Asia, esp. China
Pennisetum setaceum	Crimson Fountain Grass	Abyssinia
Pennisetum villosum	Feather Top Grass	Abyssinia
Phalaris arundinacea "Picta"	Ribbon Grass	N. America; Temperate Europe
Phalaris canariensis	Canary Grass	Mediterranean; I
Phalaris minor		Mediterranean; I
Phleum pratense	Timothy	N. America; Europe; Cultivation
Poa bulbosa	Bulbous Blue Grass	Europe; N. America
Polypogon monspeliensis	Rabbit's-foot Grass	Europe; N. America; South to Argentina

BOTANICAL NAME	COMMON NAME	ORIGIN
Rhynchelytrum roseum	Ruby Grass	South Africa; I
Scirpus tabernaemontani "Zebrinus"	Striped Bullrush	Europe
Setaria italica	Foxtail Grass	U.S. and Eurasia
Setaria palmifolia "Variegata"	Palm Grass	India
Sisyrinchium bellum	Blue-eyed Grass	N. America
Sitanion hystrix	Squirrel's-tail Grass	N. America
Sorghastrum nutans .	Indian Grass	Central N. America
Spartina pectinata "Aureo-marginata"	Cord Grass	Canada; U.S.
Stenotaphrum secundatum "Variegatum"	Striped St. Augustine Grass	Southern U.S. & Tropical America
Stipa capillata	Spear Grass	Eurasia
Stipa pennata	Feather Grass; Spear Grass	Europe
Triticum spelta	Spelt	Cultivation
Triticum sp.	Wheat	Cultivation
Uniola latifolia	Northern Sea Oats; Spangle Grass	Northeastern & Southern U.S.
Uniola paniculata	Sea Oats	Southern U.S.
Zea mays var. *japonica*	Variegated or Ornamental Corn	Central & N. America
Zizania aquatica	Wildrice	U.S.

2.
Using the Ornamental Grasses In the Garden

The use of ornamental grasses in your garden is limited primarily by the size of your property. The number of settings which are suitable for these decorative plants is endless. There are, however, those plants that grow better in shade rather than full sun, those that prefer moist rather than dry soil, etc. The plants that can fulfill special uses in the garden are listed throughout this chapter.

PERENNIAL OR SHRUB BORDERS

Perennial ornamental grasses can be placed in the landscape in the same way that shrubs are used in borders and landscape plantings around the home. The majority of the grasses form dense clumps; they do not spread by creeping rhizomes or stolons and thus may be placed in the garden just as other permanent perennial flowers and shrubs.

In considering which plant is best suited for a particular location, it is important to know the overall outline or shape of the plant. Within the ornamental grasses there are basically seven different outlines or plant forms. These are upright-narrow, upright-open, upright-arching, mound, open and spreading, tufted, and irregular. The overall form of each grass is listed in Chapter 5 in the individual descriptions and also at the end of this section on perennial borders. These seven forms are illustrated in Figure 6 (upright-open), Figure 10 (upright-narrow), Figure 20 (upright-arching), and in the photographs

Perennial Grasses can be used in home landscaping in the same manner as shrubs or small trees. Here, from the left, are Liriope muscari, 'Big Blue,' *a ground cover in the Lily family;* Miscanthus sinensis, *Japanese Silver Grass; and* Pennisetum alopecuroides, *Fountain Grass.* Photo by William Frederick.

of *Pennisetum alopecuroides* (mound), *Helictotrichon sempervirens* (tufted), *Lamarkia aurea,* (open and spreading), and *Glyceria maxima* "Variegata" (irregular). Each form indicates the particular use which the plant can have in the landscape.

Height, together with overall form and seasonal variation, are the three most important factors to consider when using an ornamental grass in a perennial border. Taller grasses, especially those that tend to lose their lower leaves, such as *Miscanthus sacchariflorus,* Eulalia Grass, look best in the background, while shorter plants demand the foreground to be noticed. Grasses that have different forms can be combined in one border to create interest or to complement other evergreen and deciduous shrubs. Fine textured evergreens, such as *Taxus*

Pennisetum alopecuroides, *Fountain Grass, forms a mound of foliage that is topped by numerous spikes of flowers in the fall. Both* Pennisetum alopecuroides *and* Pennisetum setaceum *have mound plant forms.*

Blue Oat Grass, Helictotrichon sempervirens, *is characterized by a tufted plant form. Many of the* Festuca spp. *also have tufted plant forms.*

Lamarkia aurea, *Gold Top, is an annual that typically represents the open-spreading plant form that is characteristic of some of the grasses.*

A few grasses have an irregular plant form, such as Glyceria maxima *'Variegata,' Manna Grass, illustrated above in a water garden.*

species, or Yews and *Juniperus* species, the common Juniper, form excellent backgrounds for decorative grasses. Because the grasses have such unique texture and appearance, they add new interest to the conventional shrub border.

There is no limit to the complementary effects that can be achieved with the colorful grasses and other perennial flowers. The coppery-purple spikes of *Pennisetum alopecuroides,* Fountain Grass, can be highlighted in plantings with Rudbeckia or Hemerocallis. *Helictotrichon sempervirens,* Blue Oat Grass, and *Festuca ovina* "Glauca," Dwarf Blue Fescue, both have light silvery blue foliage that make an attractive combination with purple or dark red foliage, such as *Ajuga reptans* "Atropurpurea," Bugle Weed, or *Berberis japonica* "Atropurpurea," Red Barberry. *Phalaris arundinacea* "Picta," Ribbon Grass, has long been a garden favorite in Europe due to its crisp green and white striped foliage. Bright flowers in rich red, orange, and purple tones are even more dramatic when planted in front of Ribbon Grass.

It is important to note also that the grasses flower over a considerable length of time during the growing season. An early flowering species, such as *Deschampsia caespitosa,* Tufted Hair Grass, may be planted near *Pennisetum alopecuroides,* in order that Fountain Grass will dominate when the *Deschampsia* has passed its peak in September. Early flowering bulbs, such as crocus and tulips, can be planted beside *Molinea caerulea* "Variegata," Purple Moor Grass, which begins to grow and flower in late June when it will overshadow the less attractive foliage of the spring bulbs.

The number of combinations of grasses with other perennial flowers and shrubs is truly endless. But before planting a new grass, it is wise to know its seasonal variations and landscape characteristics. These are discussed in detail in Chapter 5.

Listed below, however, are the grasses appropriate for use in a perennial or shrub border. They are subdivided by height and the abbreviated plant form directly follows each name.

TALLER GRASSES
(4' or greater) for the Background

BOTANICAL NAME	COMMON NAME	PLANT FORM
Ampelodesmos maritanicus		UO†
Arundo donax	Giant Reed	UO-UA
Arundo donax "Versicolor"	Giant Reed	UO-UA
Cortaderia selloana	Pampas Grass	UO-UN
Eragrostis curvula	Weeping Love Grass	UO-UA
Erianthus ravennae	Plume Grass	UO
Miscanthus sacchariflorus	Eulalia Grass	UN-UO
Miscanthus sacchariflorus "Giganteus"	Grant Eulalia	UN
Miscanthus sinensis	Eulalia Grass	UO
Miscanthus sinensis "Gracillimus"	Maiden Grass	UA
Miscanthus sinensis "Variegatus"	Striped Eulalia Grass	UO
Miscanthus sinensis "Zebrinus"	Zebra Grass	UN-UO
Panicum virgatum	Switch Grass	UN
Sorghastrum nutans	Indian Grass	UO
Spartina pectinata "Aureo-marginata"	Cord Grass	UA-UO
Uniola paniculata	Sea Oats	UN-UA

†PLANT FORMS
M=Mound
OS=Open-Spreading
T=Tufted
UN=Upright-narrow
UA=Upright-arching
UO=Upright-open
I=Irregular

MEDIUM GRASSES
(2–4' tall) for the Midground

BOTANICAL NAME	COMMON NAME	PLANT FORM
Andropogon scoparius	Side Oats Grama	UO
Carex buchananii	Leatherleaf Sedge Grass	UA-UN
*Carex pendula	Pendulous Sedge Grass	M-UA
Calamagrostis epigeous	Reed Grass	UN-UO
*Deschamsia caespitosa	Tufted Hair Grass	M
Eragrostis trichodes	Love Grass	UA
Glyceria maxima "Variegata"	Sweet Manna Grass	I
*Helictotrichon sempervirens	Blue Oat Grass	T
Hordeum jubatum	Squirrel's-tail Grass	UO
Hystrix patula	Bottlebrush Grass	UO
Melica altissima "Atropurpurea"	Purple Melic	UO
*Pennisetum alopecuroides	Fountain Grass	M
*Pennisetum setaceum	Crimson Fountain Grass	M
Pennisetum villosum	Feather Top Grass	I
Phalaris arundinacea "Picta"	Ribbon Grass	UO
Rhynchelytrum roseum	Ruby Grass	UO-I
Scirpus tabernaemontani "Zebrinus"	Striped Bullrush	UN
Sitanian hystrix	Squirrel's-tail Grass	UO
Stipa pennata	Feather Grass	UO
Uniola latifolia	Northern Sea Oats	UA
Zea mays "Quadricolor"	Ornamental Corn	UN
Zizania aquatica	Wildrice	UO

†PLANT FORMS
M=Mound
OS=Open-Spreading
T=Tufted
UN=Upright-narrow

UA=Upright-arching
UO=Upright-open
I=Irregular

*May also be used in the foreground

SHORT GRASSES
(2' tall or less) for the Foreground

BOTANICAL NAME	COMMON NAME	PLANT FORM
Acorus gramineus "Variegatus"	Japanese Sweet Flag	OS-I
Alopecurus pratensis "Aureus"	Meadow Foxtail	UO
Arrhenatherum elatius var. *bulbosum* "Variegatum"	Bulbous Oat Grass	UO
Bouteloua gracilis	Side Oats Grama	UO
Carex morrowii "Variegata"	Japanese Sedge Grass	M
Carex riparia "Variegata"	Pond Sedge	M
Dactylis glomerata "Variegata"	Striped Cock's-foot Grass	UO
Deschampsia flex uosa	Wavy Hair Grass	T-UO
Elymus arenarius	Blue Lyme Grass	I
Elymus glaucus	Blue Lyme Grass	I
Festuca amethystina	Large Blue Fescue	T
Festuca ovina "Glauca"	Dwarf Blue Fescue	T
Festuca ovina variants		T
Holcus lanatus "Variegatus"	Velvet Grass	OS
Holcus mollis "Variegatus"	Velvet Grass	OS
Koeleria cristata "Glauca"	June Grass	UO
Luzula spp.	White Woodrush	UA
Millium effusum "Aureum"	Golden Millet	UO
Molinea caerulea "Variegata"	Purple Moor Grass	UA
Sisyrinchium bellum	Blue-eyed Grass	I

†PLANT FORMS
M=Mound
OS=Open-Spreading
T=Tufted
UN=Upright-narrow
UA=Upright-arching
UO=Upright-open
I=Irregular

A perennial planting, in an urban location in Ithaca, New York. Grasses that have done well in poor growing conditions are from left foreground, Pennisetum alopecuroides, *Fountain Grass; background left,* Pennisetum setaceum, *Crimson Fountain Grass; behind bench,* Panicum virgatum, *Switch Grass; and foreground left, Blue Oat Grass,* Helictotrichon sempervirens.

SPECIMEN OR ACCENT PLANTS

Specimen plants are unique in that they are attractive enough to be used alone in a prominent garden area. Their uniqueness stems from distinctive flowers, foliage, or plant form that is eye-catching or sometimes even domineering. The more distinctive or domineering plants must be used with restraint or the total garden will be overshadowed by a few conspicuous specimens. *Cortaderia selloana*, Pampas Grass, is probably the most conspicuous ornamental grass because its size—up to 20 feet with 2–3-foot flowers—demands attention. But when used in a large setting with other complementary plants, Pampas Grass truly lives up to its title of "Queen of the Ornamental Grasses."

A top-notch specimen plant looks good for most, if not all, of the growing season. Some of the grasses tend to flower quickly and then become unattractive; these, of course, shouldn't be used as garden specimens.

A useful spot for a specimen or accent plant is beside the front door of a house. Not only will this attract the guests to the correct entranceway, but this allows close attention to the decorative specimen.

Large, showy grasses can be used to attract attention across an expanse of lawn, down a garden path, or to a special corner of the garden. This is not to imply, however, that specimen plants are always large. Smaller grasses placed in a conspicuous location—e.g. in containers near an outdoor living area—can also function as useful specimen plants.

Grasses which are attractive at least six months of the year and are suitable for use as specimen plants are as follows:

Acorus gramineus "Variegatus"	Japanese Sweet Flag
Alopecurus pratensis "Aureus"	Meadow Foxtail
*Arundo donax	Giant Reed
Arundo donax "Versicolor"	Striped Reed
Carex morrowii "Variegata"	Japanese Sedge Grass
**Cortaderia selloana*	Pampas Grass
Elymus arenarius	Blue Lyme Grass
Elymus glaucus	Blue Lyme Grass
**Erianthus ravennae*	Plume Grass
Festuca ovina "Glauca"	Dwarf Blue Fescue
Glyceria maxima "Variegata"	Sweet Manna Grass
Helictotrichon sempervirens	Blue Oat Grass
Holcus lanatus "Variegata"	Velvet Grass
Holcus mollis "Variegata"	Velvet Grass
**Miscanthus sacchariflorus*	Eulalia Grass
**Miscanthus sacchariflorus* "Giganteus"	Giant Eulalia
Miscanthus sinensis	Eulalia Grass

Miscanthus sinensis "Gracillimus"	Maiden Grass
Miscanthus sinensis "Variegatus"	Striped Eulalia
Miscanthus sinensis "Zebrinus"	Zebra Grass
Pennisetum alopecuroides	Fountain Grass
Pennisetum setaceum	Crimson Fountain Grass
Phalaris arundinacea "Picta"	Ribbon Grass
Scirpus tabernaemontani "Zebrinus"	Striped Bullrush
Setaria palmifolia "Variegata"	Palm Grass
Uniola latifolia	Northern Sea Oats
°Zea mays "Quadricolor"	Ornamental Corn

°May be domineering due to overall form, flowers, or foliage.

WATER GARDENS

A natural location in the garden to place grasses and many of the ornamental sedges is along the margin of a pond or stream (see color). *Arundo donax,* the very large and dramatic Giant Reed, can be a striking specimen plant near a formal (or informal) swimming pool. *Spartina pectinata* "Aureo-marginata," Cord Grass, and *Elymus arenarius,* Blue Lyme Grass, are both native to coastal areas and thus fit in very well near a stream or pond. These latter two species just mentioned, however, should be planted with caution, as they both have stout creeping rhizomes which can cause them to become a nuisance. Plant them with restraint and confine their roots with metal edging or containers which are sunken into the ground. Heavy clay soils tend to restrict the rhizomes more than light, sandy soils.

For natural ponds where a wildlife cover is desirable, *Panicum virgatum,* Switch Grass, can withstand moist soil and yet retain its upright-narrow plant form throughout the winter (Figure 14).

Shorter types which add interest to a pond or formal pool but do not detract from the pleasing horizontal effect of the water are *Acorus gramineus* "Variegatus," Japanese Sweet Flag, and *Molinea caerulea* "Variegata," Purple Moor Grass, both of which are less than 2 feet tall.

A few species can actually be planted and grown in water, such as *Scirpus taebernamontani* "Zebrinus," Striped Bullrush, *Glyceria maxima* "Variegata," Sweet Manna Grass, and *Zizania aquatica*, Wildrice.

In addition to the types mentioned above, the following plants are also suitable for water gardens or moist, wet soils:

BOTANICAL NAME	COMMON NAME
Alopecurus pratensis "Aureus"	Golden Foxtail
Arundo donax "Versicolor"	Striped Reed
Carex buchananii	Leatherleaf Sedge
Carex morrowii "Variegata"	Japanese Sedge
Carex riparia "Variegata"	Pond Sedge
Calamagrostis epigeous	Reed Grass
Coix lacryma-jobi	Job's Tears
Deschampsia caespitosa	Tufted Hair Grass
Holcus mollis "Variegatus"	Velvet Grass
Miscanthus sacchariflorus	Eulalia Grass
Miscanthus sinensis	Eulalia Grass
Miscanthus sinensis "Zebrinus"	Zebra Grass
Molinea caerulea "Variegata"	Purple Moor Grass
Phalaris arundinacea "Picta"	Ribbon Grass

GRASSES FOR SEASHORE PLANTINGS
—sandy soil with full sun.

Elymus arenarius	Blue Lyme Grass
Phalaris arundinacea "Picta"	Ribbon Grass
Spartina pectinata "Aureo-marginata"	Cord Grass
Uniola paniculata	Sea Oats

Additional grasses for the seashore, although not ornamental in all aspects:

Ammophilia arenaria	Beach Grass
Phragmites communis	Common Reed

GROUND COVERS AND ROCK GARDENS

These two garden settings are treated together because many of the grasses that are good ground cover plants are also attractive in the rock garden. Many of the grasses make excellent landscape plants for these settings because of their short, dense growth and attractive form.

Traditionally, ground covers have been creeping plants with reclining stems. A few of the grasses fall into this category, and have reclining stems in the form of rhizomes or stolons. Others, however, form dense individual tufts and are planted in combination with a decorative mulch. Plants with creeping rhizomes or stolons deserve special attention and may require containers around their roots to keep them from becoming invasive. Those that form tufts are usually spaced 1 to 2 feet apart mulched with gravel, peat moss, or wood chips. *Festuca ovina* "Glauca," Dwarf Blue Fescue, is a very popular grass for use as a ground cover or in the rock garden due to its silvery blue tufts just 6 to 8 inches tall (see color).

When using ornamental grasses in the rock garden, shorter plants are usually the most desirable. They remain in scale with the rest of the area and don't crowd or shade the other plants. Tuft- or clump-forming grasses are easier to use than those that spread by rhizomes or stolons.

Festuca ovina "Glauca," Dwarf Blue Fescue, and *Arrhenatherum elatius* var. *bulbosum* "Variegatum," Bulbous Oat Grass, are both known for their ability to grow on rocky, well-drained, dry soils which may be characteristic of some rock gardens.

In writing about grasses and ground covers, this section would not be complete without mentioning the checkerboard lawns created by South American landscape architect Burle Marx. He has planted large alternate blocks of *Stenotaphrum secundatum,* the regular green St. Augustine Grass, with *Stenotaphrum secundatum* "Variegatum," the white and green striped St. Augustine Grass, to achieve a giant checkerboard pattern of white and green squares. This is an interesting design that creates a bold landscape effect.

A rock garden is a lovely setting for the delicate Molinea caerulea 'Variegata,' *Purple Moor Grass, that grows to just 1–2' tall.*

A decorative grass for edgings or as a ground cover is Stenotaphrum *secundatum 'Variegatum,' Striped St. Augustine Grass. It's shown here as an edging along the floor of the Palm House, at Kew Botanical Gardens, England.*

GRASSES FOR GROUND COVERS AND/OR ROCK GARDENS

TYPE	FORM	GROUND COVER	ROCK GARDEN
Acorus gramineus "Variegatus"	Tufted		✿
Alopecurus pratensis "Aureus"	Tufted		✿
Arrhenatherum elatius var. *bulbosum* "Variegatum"	Tufted		✿
Bouteloua gracilis	Tufted		✿
Carex morrowii "Variegata"	Tufted	✿	✿
Carex riparia "Variegata"	Tufted	✿	✿
Deschampsia caespitosa	Tufted		✿
Deschampsia flexuosa	Tufted		✿
Festuca amethystina	Tufted	✿	✿
Festuca ovina "Glauca"	Tufted	✿	✿
Festuca ovina var. *duriuscula*	Tufted	✿	✿
Helictotrichon sempervirens	Tufted		✿
Holcus lanatus "Variegatus"	Tufted		✿
Holcus mollis "Variegatus"	Rhizomatous	✿	✿
Koeleria cristata "Glauca"	Tufted		✿
Luzulu sp.	Tufted		✿
Molinea caerulea "Variegata"	Tufted	✿	✿
Phalaris arundinacea "Picta"	Rhizomatous	✿	

TYPE	FORM	GROUND COVER	ROCK GARDEN
Sisryinchium bellum	Tufted		✽
Stenotaphrum secundatum "Variegata"	Stoloniferous	✽	✽

SCREENS

Some of the taller grasses, such as *Miscanthus sacchariflorus, Erianthus ravennae,* and *Miscanthus sinensis,* can be used as screens to enclose an outdoor living area. Because of the fast growth which these plants achieve in just a few months, they have value for temporary and attractive screens to insure privacy near a patio or backyard. They may also be used to form a visual barrier from one part of the garden to another, or to block unsightly views. They are, however, not a permanent, year-round screen and are most effective just during the growing season.

The grasses listed below are all deciduous and herbaceous. This means that in the fall and winter of the year, the stems and leaves turn brown and die; new growth begins from the base of the plant each spring. During the winter, the plants remain fairly upright and continue to provide some effect as a screen. In late winter or early spring, the previous year's growth should be cut back to within 6 to 8 inches of the ground (see Chapter 4—"Culture and Maintenance") thus removing any screen effect which the plant may have been used for. The growth in the spring is rapid, however, and by midsummer the plants are quite tall.

TALL SCREENS 8' *tall or more*

Arundo donax	Giant Reed
Cortaderia selloana	Pampas Grass
Erianthus ravennae	Plume Grass
Miscanthus sacchariflorus "Giganteus"	Giant Eulalia

MEDIUM SCREENS 5–8′ tall

Miscanthus sacchariflorus	Eulalia Grass
Miscanthus sinensis	Eulalia Grass
Miscanthus sinensis "Gracillimus"	Maiden Grass
Miscanthus sinensis "Zebrinus"	Zebra Grass
Panicum virgatum	Switch Grass (3–6′ tall)

NATURALIZED AREAS

Naturalized areas are the settings within a garden where plants appear to be growing naturally, as if they were not intentionally planted but were put there by nature. Daffodils are often naturalized along the edge of woods or garden paths. Naturalized plants grow informally, in no designed pattern, often reseed themselves, and continue to multiply after the initial placement by man.

Woodlands, meadows, vacant lots, and open fields are ideal settings to grow naturalized plants. Transition zones which exist between formal landscaped settings and the surrounding informal areas can be developed as naturalized areas. Thus, if a backyard was adjacent to a woodlot, naturalized plants could be placed along the edge of the yard to link the woods or informal area with the landscaped formal area or yard.

Plants especially suited for these informal, natural areas should be easy to grow, attractive, yet not necessarily conspicuous, and require little, if any maintenance.

Many of the ornamental grasses are excellent plants to naturalize for either sunny or shady locations. *Uniola latifolia*, Northern Sea Oats, and *Hystrix patula*, Bottlebrush Grass, are ideal grasses to naturalize in shady woods (Figure 9). Both have decorative flowers and form clumps 2 to 4 feet tall. *Andropogon scoparius*, Little Bluestem, and *Bouteloua gracilis*, Side Oats Grama, are two short decorative grasses which can be directly seeded where they are to naturalize. Both of these are especially suited to grow in meadows or open fields, and are short enough that they can be planted as a substitute for turf grass. Little Bluestem can grow to 2 feet tall while Side Oats Grama remains about 12 to 18 inches tall. These two plants can be seeded in combination in an area along the edge of a lawn to form an attractive natural "meadow" that requires minimal maintenance. Unlike a lawn, these grasses need only be mowed once or twice a year.

Listed below are additional ornamental grasses that can be naturalized, along with the location best suited for each type.

GRASSES FOR NATURALIZED AREAS

TYPE	COMMON NAME	LOCATION
Andropogon scoparius	Little Bluestem	Sun
Bouteloua gracilis	Mosquito Grass or Side Oats Grama	Sun
Briza media	Quaking Grass	Sun/Shade
Deschampsia caespitosa	Tufted Hair Grass	Sun/Shade
Eragrostis curvula	Weeping Love Grass	Sun
Eragrostis trichodes	Sand Love Grass	Sun
Festuca gigantea	Giant Fescue	Sun/Shade
Hystrix patula	Bottlebrush Grass	Shade
Luzula sp.	White Woodrush	Shade
Miscanthus sacchariflorus	Eulalia Grass	Sun
Miscanthus sinensis	Eulalia Grass	Sun
Panicum virgatum	Switch Grass	Sun
Phalaris canariensis	Canary Grass	Sun
Sisryinchium bellum	Blue-eyed Grass	Sun/Shade
Sorghastrum nutans	Indian Grass	Sun
Spartina pectinata "Aureo-marginata"	Cord Grass	Sun
Uniola latifolia	Northern Sea Oats	Shade
Uniola paniculata	Sea Oats	Sun

ANNUAL BORDERS

Showy, annual grasses, grown primarily for their cut flowers, can add a whole new dimension to the annual border. The flowers range in color from the ruby red or purple of *Rhynchelytrum roseum*, Ruby Grass, to the pale green or ivory *Lagurus ovatus*, Hare's-tail Grass. Some of these annuals flower profusely for a short time, then often quite quickly begin to turn brown and die. They simply have a short life cycle and after flowering many species are no longer attractive for landscaping purposes. There are, however, a few types which remain attractive throughout most of the summer, especially if the plants are not started indoors early in spring, but are directly seeded outdoors when the growing season begins (see color).

The short-lived types are best suited for the vegetable or flower garden, where the plants are grown in rows and the flowers can be cut for arrangements. Many of the cultivated cereal grasses such as Wheat, Oats, Millet, Timothy, etc. are grown for their ornamental flowers. Because these plants have no landscape value, they are characteristic of the grasses to be grown in the vegetable garden.

The longer-lasting annual grasses offer a wide variety of colors and textures to use in the traditional flower border. The tawny color of *Apera spica-venti*, Loose Silky Bent Grass, with its open, finely branched panicles is a light, decorative addition to the garden. *Pennisetum setaceum*, Crimson Fountain Grass, and *Pennisetum villosum*, Feather Top Grass, are grown as annuals in cool climates (USDA Zone 8 and Northward) for their dense, spike-like flowers that are purple and white respectively. These two species of *Pennisetum* and *Rhynchelytrum roseum*, Ruby Grass, should be started from seed indoors in early spring if they are to be grown in the North because these types require a fairly long growing season.

Ornamental Corn, *Zea mays* "Quadricolor," and Job's Tears, *Coix lacryma-jobi*, are both plants with coarse-textured foliage.

Although they remain colorful for most of the summer, the plants are conspicuous and require a special place in the landscape. They are more or less curiosity plants, and although Ornamental Corn does have decorative foliage (pink, yellow, white, and green striped), consideration should be given to planting these grasses where they will not overshadow other decorative species.

In contrast to such coarse texture, *Aira capillaris* var. *pulchella*, Hair Grass, and *Agrostis nebulosa*, Cloud Grass, are the ultimate in fine textured plants. When grown in a border, they should be spaced no more than 6 inches apart. When in flower, the branched panicles along with the leaves are so fine and slender that the entire planting resembles a light green cloud, or mist. A large number (50) of the plants should be grouped together to achieve the best results. Hair Grass and Cloud Grass, however, rarely are attractive all summer long. When they begin to turn brown and the flowers disarticulate (fall apart), the plants should be removed and others put in their place. They are well worth the effort, however, for no other plant can create such a fine, cloud-like textural effect.

When planting grasses in the annual border, they are spaced according to height. Smaller types, such as *Sisyrinchium bellum*, Blue-eyed Grass, can be spaced 6 inches apart or less, while *Apera spica-venti*, Loose Silky Bent Grass, requires a 12-inch spacing between plants. In a grouping for landscaping purposes, the plants can be placed closer together to achieve a mass effect, whereas in the vegetable or cut flower garden, the plants require more room to develop.

Listed below are the annual grasses that are best suited for flower gardens. Because of the variation in flowering period and thus decorative use in the landscape, the grasses are cateegorized by short, medium, or long flowering periods. Short (S) is attractive for 6 weeks or less, Medium (M) is attractive for 6 to 10 weeks, and Long (L) is attractive for longer than 10 weeks.

GRASSES FOR ANNUAL BORDERS

TYPE	COMMON NAME	FLOWERING PERIOD
Agrostis nebulosa	Cloud Grass	S-M
Aira capillaris var. *pulchella*	Hair Grass	S
Apera interrupta	Dense Silky Bent Grass	M
Apera spica-venti	Loose Silky Bent Grass	M
Avena fatua	Wild Oats	S
Avena sterilis	Animated Oats	S
Briza maxima	Big Quaking Grass	M
Briza minor	Little Quaking Grass	S
Bromus macrostachys	Brome Grass	M
Bromus madritensis	Brome Grass	M
Bromus sp.	Brome Grass	M
Coix lacryma-jobi	Job's Tears	L
Desmazeria sicula		M
Eragrostis abyssinica	Love Grass	L
Hordeum vulgare	Barley	M
Lagurus ovatus	Hare's-tail Grass	L
Lamarkia aurea	Golden Top	M
Pennisetum setaceum	Crimson Fountain Grass	L
Pennisetum villosum	Feather Top Grass	L
Phalaris canariensis	Canary Grass	S
Phalaris minor		S
Pheleum pratensis	Timothy	M
Polypogon monspeliensis	Rabbit's-foot Grass	M
Rhynchelytrum roseum	Ruby Grass	L
Setaria italica	Foxtail Grass	S
Sisyrinchium bellum	Blue-eyed Grass	L
Triticum spelta	Spelt	S
Triticum sp.	Wheat	S
Zea mays "Quadricolor"	Ornamental Corn	L

SPECIAL LISTS OF GRASSES

Foliage color: The foliage color of the ornamental grasses is considered to be one of their most attractive features for landscaping. The variations that exist are listed below.

BLUE OR BLUE-GRAY FOLIAGE

Elymus arenarius	Blue Lyme Grass
Elymus glaucus	Blue Lyme Grass
Festuca amethystina	Large Blue Fescue
Festuca ovina "Glauca"	Dwarf Blue Fescue
Festuca ovina var. *duriuscula*	Hard Fescue
Helictotrichon sempervirens	Blue Oat Grass
Koeleria cristata "Glauca"	June Grass

STRIPED FOLIAGE

Longitudinal white or yellow stripes:

Acorus gramineus "Variegatus"	Japanese Sweet Flag
Alopecurus pratensis "Aureus"	Meadow Foxtail
Arrhenatherum elatius var. *bulbosum* "Variegatum"	Bulbous Oat Grass
Arundo donax "Versicolor"	Striped Reed
Carex morrowii "Variegata"	Japanese Sedge Grass
Carex riparia "Variegata"	Pond Sedge
Dactylis glomerata "Variegata"	Striped Cock's-foot Grass
Glyceria maxima	Sweet Manna Grass
Holcus lanatus "Variegatus"	Velvet Grass
Holcus mollis "Variegatus"	Velvet Grass
Millium effusum "Aureum"	Millet Grass
Miscanthus sinensis "Variegatus"	Striped Eulalia

Molinea caerulea "Variegata"	Purple Moor Grass
Phalaris arundinacea "Picta"	Ribbon Grass
Setaria palmifolia	Palm Grass
Spartina pectinata "Aureo marginata"	Cord Grass
Stenotaphrum secundatum "Variegatum"	Striped St. Augustine Grass
Zea mays "Quadricolor"	Ornamental Corn

Horizontal yellow or white stripes:

Miscanthus sinensis "Zebrinus"	Zebra Grass
Scirpus tabernaemontani "Zebrinus"	Striped Bullrush

EVERGREEN OR SEMI-EVERGREEN GRASSES

Not all of the grasses are deciduous; some have attractive foliage year-round. This list has been compiled from data collected in the Northeast, it should be kept in mind that these grasses are evergreen or semi-evergreen as far north as USDA Zone 5.

Carex pendula	Pendulous Sedge Grass
Carex riparia "Variegata"	Pond Sedge
Deschampsia caespitosa	Tufted Hair Grass
Festuca amethystina	Large Blue Fescue
Festuca ovina "Glauca"	Dwarf Blue Fescue
Festuca ovina var. *duriuscula*	Hard Fescue
Helictotrichon sempervirens	Blue Oat Grass
Holcus lanatus "Variegatus"	Velvet Grass
Holcus mollis "Variegatus"	Velvet Grass
Koeleria cristata "Glauca"	June Grass

The white and green striped foliage of Miscanthus sinensis 'Variegatus,' *Striped Eulalia Grass, is colorful from early spring until late fall.*

Evergreen year-round when grown indoors:

Acorus gramineus "Variegatus"	Japanese Sweet Flag
Arrhenatherum elatius var. *bulbosum* "Variegatum"	Bulbous Oat Grass
Carex morrowii "Variegata"	Japanese Sedge Grass
Carex riparia "Variegata"	Pond Sedge
Oplismenus compositus "Vittatus"	Basket Grass
Setaria palmifolia	Palm Grass

FALL COLOR

Several grasses, especially when grown in the Northeast, turn attractive colors in autumn (see color). This, of course, provides an additional season of interest in the garden. The extent of fall color varies from year to year, as it does for trees and shrubs, depending on weather conditions. The peak of color usually comes in October and, although it varies from species to species, the coloration can last well into November or even early winter. In those areas of the United States where autumn color isn't as pronounced, the grasses that are deciduous turn beige or tan as the weather becomes colder in fall and winter. Listed below are the grasses that can exhibit fall color.

TYPE	COMMON NAME	COLOR
Andropogon scoparius	Little Bluestem	Dk. Red or Purple
Miscanthus sacchariflorus	Eulalia Grass	Orange
Panicum virgatum	Switch Grass	Yellow
Pennisetum alopecuroides	Fountain Grass	Yellow or Beige
Sorghastrum nutans	Indian Grass	Dk. Orange or Purple
Spartina pectinata "Aureo-marginata"	Cord Grass	Yellow
Uniola lalifolia	Northern Sea Oats	Bronze

GRASSES FOR SHADY LOCATIONS

Carex pendula	Pendulous Sedge Grass
Carex riparia "Variegata"	Pond Sedge
Calamagrostis epigeous	Reed Grass
Coix lacryma-jobi	Job's Tears
Deschampsia caespitosa	Tufted Hair Grass
Deschampsia flexuosa	Wavy Hair Grass
Festuca gigantea	Giant Fescue
Hystrix patula	Bottlebrush Grass
Luzula sp.	White Woodrush
Melica altissima "Atropurpurea"	Purple Melic
Millium effusum "Aureum"	Millet Grass
Molinea caerulea "Variegata"	Purple Moor Grass
Stipa pennata	Feather Grass
Uniola latifolia	Northern Sea Oats

GRASSES WITH CREEPING RHIZOMES OR STOLONS

Arundo donax	Giant Reed
Arundo donax "Versicolor"	Striped Reed (More confined than the species)
Elymus arenarius	Blue Lyme Grass
Elymus interruptus	Nodding Wild Rye
Holcus mollis "Variegatus"	Velvet Grass
Miscanthus sacchariflorus	Eulalia Grass
Oplismenus compositus "Vittatus"	Basket Grass
Phalaris arundinacea "Picta"	Ribbon Grass
Spartina pectinata "Aureomarginata"	Cord Grass
Uniola paniculata	Sea Oats

3.
Using
the Grasses as
Cut Flowers

Although the major part of this book is devoted to using the grasses as new and different landscape plants, the use of ornamental grass flowers for arrangements is by no means a secondary or supplementary subject. Long before most of the grasses were considered for landscaping, their flowers could be found in dried arrangements in florist shops throughout the United States.

In the past few years, these graceful and very naturalistic flowers have achieved even greater popularity. They are featured in huge mass arrangements in department stores, in display windows, and wherever flower arrangements are used, from table centerpieces to formal arrangements to wedding bouquets.

The grass flowers are shades of green, brown, or white in color. These natural tones lend themselves perfectly for use with other wildflowers or in naturalistic bouquets.

The flowers themselves vary widely in form and texture. By far the best known type is Pampas Grass, *Cortaderia selloana*. One or two of its 2-to-3-foot feathery white plumes literally create an arrangement by themselves. Two others that have feathery, plume-like flowers (often erroneously referred to as Pampas Grass) are Plume Grass, *Erianthus ravennae* (Figure 6) and the *Miscanthus* species, Eulalia Grass.

The dense, spike-like flowers of the Pennisetum genus (Figure 16) resemble very fine bottle brushes in purple and bronze

Figure 1. The annual grasses make ideal dried arrangements. Eleven of the most popular are shown here.

1. *Aira capillaris* var. *pulchella*
   Hair Grass
2. *Apera spica-venti*
   Loose Silky Bent Grass
3. *Bouteloua gracilis*
   Side Oats Grama
4. *Briza maxima*
   Large Quaking Grass
5. *Briza media*
   Quaking Grass
6. *Briza minor*
   Little Quaking Grass
7. *Bromus macrostachys*
   Brome Grass
8. *Eragrostis trichodes*
   Sand Love Grass
9. *Lagurus ovatus*
   Hare's Tail Grass
10. *Polypogon monospeliensis*
    Rabbit's Foot Grass
11. Rhynchelytrum roseum
    Ruby Grass

tones. The true Bottlebrush Grass is *Hystrix patula* with stiff, coarse spikes of flowers.

The renowned Sea Oats of the Southern United States, *Uniola paniculata,* is a lovely grass for dried bouquets. Its flowers are dense, slightly nodding, and pale beige. *Uniola latifolia,* Spangle Grass or Northern Sea Oats, has loose nodding flowers which turn a rich bronze color in the fall.

The *Eragrostis* species or Love Grasses can add line or form to any arrangement. Their slender, curved panicles resemble a fine textured form of Scotch Broom, *Cytisus* species.

The *Briza* genus, Quaking Grasses, have been used for hundreds of years in bouquets. The tiny florets come in three sizes, small, *Briza minor*; medium, *Briza media*; and large, *Briza maxima.* The slightest breeze will cause the flowers to shiver or quake, thus their common name. Because of their inflated, papery appearance, they are sometimes called Puffed Wheat.

Baby's Breath, *Gypsophila* species, a popular flower for dried bouquets, has a miniature counterpart of *Aira capillaris* var. *pulchella,* Hair Grass, and *Agrostis nebulosa,* Cloud Grass. These extremely delicate grasses are so fine in texture that they add a cloud-like background to an arrangement.

Hare's-tail Grass, *Lagurus ovatus,* and Rabbit's-tail Grass, *Polypogon monspeliensis,* are two favorites for display. Both have soft, dense flowers indicative of their common names.

The number of grass flowers suitable for arrangements is endless. Many of the native types, all too often referred to as "weeds," provide lovely flowers for drying which can be picked all summer long. The native types include *Setaria* species, Foxtail; *Bromus* species, Brome Grass; *Panicum* species, Switch Grass; and *Phragmites communis,* Common Reed. These grasses can be found in waste places and along roadsides in many parts of the country.

The ornamental grasses with decorative flowers are listed below (see also Figure 1).

BOTANICAL NAME	COMMON NAME
Agrostis nebulosa	Cloud Grass
Aira capillaris var. *pulchella*	Hair Grass
Ampelodesmos mauritanicus	
Andropogon scoparius	Little Bluestem
Apera interrupta	Dense Silky Bent
Apera spica-venti	Loose Silky Bent
Arundo donax	Giant Reed
Avena fatua	Wild Oats
Avena sterilis	Animated Oats
Bouteloua gracilis	Side Oats Grama
Briza maxima	Large Quaking Grass
Briza media	Quaking Grass
Briza minor	Small Quaking Grass
Bromus macrostachys	Brome Grass
Bromus madritensis	Brome Grass
Bromus sp.	Brome Grass
Calamagrostis epigeous	Reed Grass
Cortaderia selloana	Pampas Grass
Deschampsia caespitosa	Tufted Hair Grass
Deschampsia flexuosa	Wavy Hair Grass
Desmazeria sicula	Spike Grass
Elymus interruptus	Nodding Lyme Grass
Eragrostis abyssinica	Love Grass
Eragrostis curvula	Weeping Love Grass
Eragrostis trichodes	Love Grass
Erianthus ravennae	Plume Grass
*Hordeum jubatum	Squirrel's-tail Grass
Hordeum vulgare	Barley
**Hystrix patula	Bottlebrush Grass
Lagurus ovatus	Hare's-tail Grass
*Lamarkia aurea	Golden Top
Luzula sp.	White Woodrush
Millium effusum	Millet Grass
Millium effusum "Aureum"	Millet Grass

BOTANICAL NAME	COMMON NAME
Miscanthus sacchariflorus	Eulalia Grass
Miscanthus sacchariflorus "Giganteus"	Eulalia Grass
Miscanthus sinensis	Eulalia Grass
Miscanthus sinensis "Gracillimus"	Maiden Grass
Miscanthus sinensis "Variegatus"	Striped Eulalia Grass
Miscanthus sinensis "Zebrinus"	Zebra Grass
Panicum virgatum	Switch Grass
**Pennisetum alopecuroides*	Fountain Grass
**Pennisetum setaceum*	Crimson Fountain Grass
**Pennisetum villosum*	Feather Top
Phalaris canariensis	Canary Grass
Phalaris minor	
Phleum pratensis	Timothy
Polypogon monspeliensis	Rabbit's-tail Grass
Rhynchelytrum roseum	Ruby Grass
Setaria italica	Foxtail Millet
Sitanion hystrix	Squirrel's-tail Grass
Sorghastrum nutans	Indian Grass
Spartina pectinata "Aureo-marginata"	Cord Grass
Stipa capillata	Spear Grass
Stipa pennata	Feather Grass
Triticum spelta	Spelt
Triticum sp.	Wheat
Uniola latifolia	Spangle Grass, Northern Sea Oats
Uniola paniculata	Sea Oats
Zizania aquatica	Wild Rice

*Shatter easily, very difficult to use in permanent arrangements.
**May shatter if not picked early enough, and can still fall apart after dry.

PICKING THE FLOWERS

Most of the grasses are used as dried flowers in arrangements. *Rhynchelytrum roseum*, Ruby Grass, however, is one exception that looks best in fresh arrangements because its ruby red flowers fade when dried.

The most critical factor in obtaining good, everlasting cut flowers is to pick the flower just as it is expanding from the leaves of the plant. While this may seem to be an early or immature stage, it is the only means of assuring that the flower will not shatter as it dries. The longer the flowers are left on the plant the more mature the seeds become and the more likely that the seeds will fall apart as the entire head dries out. When the tiny anthers (male flower parts that bear pollen) become visible, this is a sign that pollination is occurring and from that day onward the seed will be forming. Therefore, once the male anthers appear it is an indication of the peak flowering period and a sign to then pick the flower, if not earlier.

As the seeds mature, the flowers often shatter to assure seed dispersal, for this is the built-in means of perpetuation of the species. However, not all grasses disarticulate (fall apart) at the same rate; some fall apart earlier in their life cycle than others. For instance, *Lamarkia aurea*, Golden Top, is a pretty yellow grass, but the entire flower, including the main stem, shatters at maturity, making it a very temporary specimen for dried arrangements. *Hordeum jubatum*, Squirrel's-tail Grass, and *Rhynchelytrum roseum*, Ruby Grass, are two other grasses which rarely remain intact for long-term use. Even when picked early in their life cycle, the flowers still shatter easily.

The vast majority of species, however, do not shatter when picked correctly. Remember, the earlier the flower is picked, the longer it will last for arrangements.

DRYING THE FLOWERS

The reason so many of the grasses are excellent for cut flowers is because the cut and dried flower looks almost identical to the fresh flower as it is borne on the plant. The shape, texture, and usually the color remain unchanged throughout the drying process and for years to come.

The grasses are generally wind-pollinated, and thus they have no temporary colorful flowers to attract insects or bees for pollination. With no temporary delicate flowers to fade and wither when dried, the green flowers are durable and more permanent in their duration.

Drying these flowers does not require any special or time-consuming process. The most satisfactory method of drying is to simply hang the flowers upside down in a cool, well-circulated, dry, dark room. High temperatures can cause shattering; sunlight can cause fading of the natural colors. Curved stems can be obtained by placing the cut flowers upright in a wide-mouth container (with *no* water) with the same room conditions.

The flowers usually dry in 7 to 14 days. When the stems are firm and brittle, the decorative grasses are ready to use in arrangements.

Avoid grouping a large number of stems together to dry, especially if they are placed in a container where mildew and molds can readily occur. Good ventilation should be maintained around the entire stem and flower.

Check the bunches of stems which are hung to dry every day or so. Often the stems will shrink and slip out of the string by which they are hanging.

Depending on the particular species, the leaves may or may not be removed for drying. *Miscanthus sinensis "Gracillimus,"* Maiden Grass, achieves a great deal of its form in an arrangement from its curled, graceful leaves. *Erianthus ravennae,* Plume Grass, also has attractive leaves for dried bouquets. Usually the smaller flowers, such as *Lagarus ovatus,* Hare's-tail Grass, and *Briza* species have insignificant leaves which can be cut from the stem either before or after drying.

Many of the large perennial grasses have decorative flowers that, even in their natural color, make a beautiful bouquet. Shown here are *Erianthus, Miscanthus, Uniola* and *Ampelodesmos.*

Some grasses change color, depending on their age. *Briza media*, Quaking Grass, has pale green flowers in early spring which change to beige or tan by midsummer if left on the plant. By picking this type in early spring and summer, two different colors of the same flower can be obtained. (In this case, *Briza media* doesn't shatter easily and can be picked throughout the season.)

Once the flowers are completely dry, they can be used in arrangements or bouquets. If the flowers are left in their natural color, they look best if used with other natural tones of beige, brown, and green. They can be highlighted with muted orange and red colors. If the flowers are dyed bright colors, they can be coordinated with many more room settings and decorations.

Natural grasses look best in containers which are informal and simple in design. Earthenware pots and pottery and old-fashioned crocks and baskets are especially well-suited for grass arrangements.

Other flowers and seed pods such as cattails, yarrow, money plant, teasels, Baby's Breath, strawflowers, and many of the wild flowers are especially well-suited for use with the grasses.

It is not advisable to mix fresh with dried flowers, for the dried material will easily deteriorate if used in water.

DYEING THE GRASSES

There has been considerable interest in dyeing the flowers of ornamental grasses to change their natural tones to bright vivid colors. Depending on the container to be used, location of the arrangement, and personal taste, the dyed material may be preferable to natural colors or vice versa.

The actual technique involved in dyeing flowers is acquired over a period of time and takes a great amount of patience and perseverence.

Each type of grass flower is different and thus requires specific considerations when being dyed. Any of the grasses listed in the previous table for ornamental flowers can be dyed; however, some types are more attractive than others.

There are several methods for dyeing grass flowers, the most satisfactory of which is the hot water dip dye technique. Other methods such as spray painting and uptake of colored water solutions may be succesful on other flowers, but for grasses, the hot water dip method is preferred. This is especially true when working with fluffy, light flowers, such as Pampas Grass, *Cortaderia selloana,* and Plume Grass, *Erianthus ravennae.*

Because the grass flowers dry so readily when cut, it is unlikely that they can take up enough colored water to change the flower color. Using spray paint for dyeing leaves a heavy coat of paint particles (easily visible) on the small flowers and the force of the spray can cause some of the fluffier flowers to stick together, thus losing their light natural appearance. Also, it is difficult to spray the paint to cover all surfaces of the flower and stem adequately.

The hot water dip method consists of dissolving a strong dye along with a mordant in boiling water. The flowers are then dipped (upside down) into the boiling solution, and depending on the type of flower, left until they turn color.

A suitable strong dye may be difficult for the average consumer to obtain. The ideal chemicals are aniline dyes, used by commercial firms and universities in staining slides, especially for biology laboratories. These dyes come in various colors ranging from yellow and orange through green, blue, and purple. They are usually sold in powdered form and are quite strong dyes.

A substitute for the aniline chemicals, however, are clothing dyes readily available in department stores. Clothing dyes can result in dull heavy colors, especially if dark colors are used; light, bright colors usually give the best results.

Another type of dye which is suitable for changing flower color is stamp pad ink. This is the liquid ink that is sold in stationery and book stores for refilling stamp pads. The colors of this ink are somewhat limited, usually to blue, green, and red.

A mordant should be included in the boiling mixture to "fix" the dye. The mordant allows the actual dye coloring to become available and adhere to the flower. Some of the more common mordants are alum (potassium alum in preference to ammonium alum), stannous chloride and acetic acid (regular vinegar). Alum is available in powdered form from drugstores.

The exact amount of mordant and dye used may vary, depending on the type of dye and the flowers being used. The aniline chemicals are quite potent and require only a small amount (less than a tablespoon) for a strong concentration. Clothing dyes, however, especially the liquid form, have to be used at higher rates (½ cup), whereas one bottle (1.2 oz.) of stamp pad ink is necessary for each pint of dye solution.

Soft water has been shown to give better results than hard water in obtaining good dyed flowers.

Th following recipes should be used only as guidelines for dyeing. Depending on the type of flower, temperature of water, etc., the amounts of dye and mordant may vary.

ANILINE DYE SOLUTION
For every 1 quart of water use:
> ½ teaspoon aniline dye, and
> 8 teaspoons alum *or* 1 teaspoon acetic acid

CLOTHING DYE SOLUTION
For every 1 quart of water use:
> 2–4 oz. clothing dye, and
> 8 teaspoons alum *or* 1 teaspoon acetic acid

STAMP PAD INK SOLUTION
For every 1 quart of water use:
> 2 1.2-oz. bottles of ink and
> 8 teaspoons alum *or* 1 teaspoon acetic acid

To prepare flowers for dyeing, make sure they are clean, intact (not shattering) specimens. The less color in the flower, the easier the dye will noticeably penetrate; for instance, beige or pale ivory heads will change quicker than green or bronze heads. Recently picked specimens may dye quicker; however, their weak, lax stems may not be stiff enough to hold up in the hot water. Many of the plants that have dry papery flowers, the *Briza* species and the *Uniola* species, have the same dry texture whether freshly cut or dried for months. Therefore, it makes little difference if the flowers are fresh or dried when dyed. Dried material may be easier to work with.

It is best to use a deep, narrow container to dye the flowers, so that the heads as well as the stems can be dipped into the solution.

Dissolve the mordant (alum or acetic acid) in water and heat to boiling, then add the dye. Continue to keep the solution hot (about 200°F, not necessarily at a full boil or the flowers may break apart) while dyeing the flowers. Holding the heads upside down, dip them into the solution and leave until the color has penetrated the grass. This may take just a few seconds, as in the case of *Aira capillaris* var. *pulchella*, Hair Grass, to much longer for *Briza maxima*, Large Quaking Grass. Learning how much time is required to dye different flowers is one of the major keys to mastering the dyeing technique.

Once the flowers have changed color, remove them from the solution and gently tap off the excess moisture. Lay the heads on newspaper, or hang them upside down to drip dry (1 to 2 days).

When light feathery flowers (e.g. Pampas Grass, *Cortaderia selloana*, and Hare's-tail Grass, *Lagurus ocatus*) are dipped in the dye, they become dense and matted down. After the color has penetrated these flowers, gently tap off the excess water and shake the plumes. By hanging them upside down to dry and gently shaking the heads, they will regain their fluffy appearance.

Dye solutions, especially the stamp pad mixture, may lose their potency after a few months, so it is best to mix a fresh batch of solution each time, rather than keeping it from year to year.

Once dyed, the flowers will retain their bright color for years, and can be used in a wide variety of arrangements.

4.
Culture
and
Maintenance

Ornamental grasses usually require minimal care throughout the growing season. When the plants are placed in fertile, well-drained soil, they flourish and need no special care. In general, they can be treated just as shrubs or large herbaceous perennials. An annual fertilization of 1–2 lbs. 5-10-10 or 5-10-5 per 100 square feet should be adequate. Insects and diseases are rarely a problem. The exact cultural practices vary depending on the plant's duration, either annual (horticultural annuals are included here) or perennial.

ANNUALS AND HORTICULTURAL ANNUALS

Annual grasses, as well as those plants grown as annuals in colder regions of the U.S., are grown from seed each year. For earlier flowering, the plants can be started indoors, or the seed can be sown directly in the garden after the danger of frost is past in the spring. Allow 3 to 5 weeks for the seed to germinate and grow indoors before planting outside. The correct spacing for most annuals is 6 to 12 inches apart. Almost all of the annual grasses prefer full sun and require only adequate moisture and fertile soil for good growth. Seed can be collected from the plants and saved for planting the following season, for none of the grasses are hybrids. The seed is mature and fully ripe when it begins to fall off the plant. For storage through the winter, place the seed in a dry, well-circulated area where it will not freeze. Seed stored for more than one year will have a much lower percentage of germination.

When sowing the seed of annual grasses in the garden, it is a good idea to mark the area with a row of string. When the grasses germinate, the tiny plants may be confused with other grass weeds in the garden, if they are not marked at the time of planting. When the plants are 1 to 2 inches tall, thin them to 6 to 12 inches apart. Taller annuals, such as *Apera spica-venti*, Loose Silky Bent Grass, require about a 1-foot spacing, while shorter types, such as *Lagurus ovatus*, Hare's-tail Grass, can be spaced 6 inches apart.

If the growing conditions are hot and dry, it will be helpful to keep the grasses well-watered. After the plants begin to flower, they can easily turn brown and die from lack of adequate soil moisture.

As far as maintenance is concerned, annual grasses require periodic weeding through the summer, and, of course, need to be reseeded each year. Some of the annuals that have a short life cycle, where they flower and go to seed quickly, can self-sow in the garden and become a nuisance. *Aira capillaris* var. *pulchella*, Hair Grass, *Apera spica-venti*, the *Bromus* species, Brome Grass, may be troublesome in this way. The best means of controlling this is to keep the flowers picked from the plants and not to give them a chance to shed their seed in the garden.

PERENNIALS

Perennial grasses are usually purchased as plants, but they can be grown from seed. When plants are used, they grow to their mature size in 1 to 2 years, whereas plants from seed may take 3 to 5 years to reach maturity and flower. Spacing for the plants depends upon their purpose in the landscape and the type of plant. A rule of thumb is the spacing should equal the mature height of the plant. For landscape plantings, however, this distance may often be too far apart. In any case, the mature height should be considered.

Perennial grasses should be planted in the same way as shrubs or small trees. In warm or mild climates planting can be done in spring or fall; in colder climates (USDA Zone 5 and farther north) planting should be done in the spring. Dig a hole 1½ times the size of the root ball. Improve the excavated soil by adding equal parts of peat moss, manure, or other organic matter and sand to form a ratio of 1 part soil, 1 part organic matter, and 1 part sand. The only fertilizer necessary at the time of planting is super-phosphate (0-20-0), which should be added to the improved backfill soil at the rate of 2 tablespoons per bushel. After placing the plant in the prepared hole, fill and firm the improved soil around the roots. Never plant the grass deeper than it was growing in the nursery or cover more than 1 inch of soil on top of the original root ball. Leave a saucer-like basin around the plant so that water will run toward the main stem and not away from it. After a thorough watering, mulch the plant with loose organic matter (peat moss, chopped leaves, bark).

Although many of the perennials will grow in a variety of locations, check the individual listings in Chapter 5 to be sure that plants being located in a particular site will actually grow and do well there.

ANNUAL PRUNING AND DIVISION

There are two maintenance practices which are required when growing perennial grasses. These are, first, cutting the plants back to the ground each year, and second, occasional division of the plants. The large perennials form dense thick clumps of new growth which begins at the base of the plant each year. By the fall of the year, the plants have reached their mature height and although the leaves turn brown and growth stops, the plants remain upright. In the spring, as new growth starts, the brown stems and leaves from the previous year are still present. Removing the previous year's growth in early spring insures more vigorous new growth, acts as a pruning method to remove any diseased or dead stems, and helps to create a more attractive plant. A great many of the grasses are especially attractive in the fall and early winter. At this time the large feathery flowers are in full bloom and at their peak of showiness. Therefore, it is best to carry out any cultural practices, such as annual pruning, in late winter or early spring. At this time, the larger grasses can be cut back to within 6 inches of the ground with large pruning shears. The smaller grasses can be pruned with hand clippers, or sometimes the old stems and leaves can be simply raked away from the base of the plant.

Occasionally, division of the perennial grasses may be neces-

Before annual pruning in late winter, Fountain Grass, Pennisetum alopecuroides, *remains upright, but is totally brown and unattractive.*

After pruning, the same plant as the previous photo, cut back to within 6″ of the ground.

New growth is initiated from the base each year on the deciduous perennial grasses. This is the same plant of Fountain Grass the summer after pruning.

sary in order to keep the plants healthy and profusely flowering. Division involves digging the entire plant and dividing it into several smaller plants. Perhaps the grass that benefits most from this practice is Dwarf Blue Fescue, *Festuca ovina* var. "Glauca." This short, blue-gray grass may have a tendency to "die out" in the center of the plant, especially if grown in heavy, poorly drained soils in warm climates. Thus, the plants require division every one or two years in order to keep the entire plant alive and growing.

Division of the other perennial grasses should occur about every 5 to 10 years. Some species çan grow in one place for several years and actually look their best when allowed to do so. All divisions should be made when the plants are dormant or just beginning to grow in early spring. The need for division is determined by the appearance of the new growth in the spring. If a plant shows signs of growth only around the edges and not in the center, the middle of the plant is probably dead and the plant should be dug and divided. Grasses which show uniform new growth can be left in place for a longer period of time.

When dividing a plant, remove it entirely from the soil, retaining as many roots as possible. Try to dig the plant just after new leaves have appeared in the spring, in order to see the extent of healthy active growth. The size of the plant determines how many smaller plants can be cut from the main clump. Discard any dead portions and divide the green, healthy new growth in several equal pieces. A 5- to 10-year-old plant of *Pennisetum alopecuroides*, Fountain Grass, can be divided into 4 or 5 good-sized new smaller plants.

Probably the most difficult part of dividing an ornamental grass is the actual separation of the plants, once they are dug. The older grasses form such dense tight root systems that they may be very difficult to break apart. An axe and a very strong arm may be the best method, as a shovel is usually not strong enough. A hacksaw may also be helpful.

STAKING

Only one other cultural practice may be required when growing perennial grasses. In some cases, the larger types may require staking for support of the flowering stems. This is especially true if the plants are grown in very fertile soil in shady locations. All of the *Miscanthus* species prefer full sun, and when grown in rich soils where the plants are in shade for half of the day or more, the tall stems seem to collapse easily. Staking by using 1 to 2 tall, sturdy posts with string holding the plants upright can be a nuisance and may appear unattractive, if not tastefully concealed. It is best to consider the soil type and location previous to selecting the ornamental grass to be placed in a particular location.

A large plant of Miscanthus sinensis 'Gracillimus,' Maiden Grass, is removed for division. With the larger perennials division is necessary every 5–10 years.

The single plant specimen prior to division.

The actual division of the root system is often difficult because the grasses form very dense clumps. Here, an axe is the best tool to use for separating the roots.

Only two plants were obtained from this division, and one is being replanted above. Mature clumps can often be separated into four or more good-sized plants. For ease of handling, the annual pruning of the foliage was completed after division.

INTERIOR ORNAMENTAL GRASSES

The grasses that can be grown indoors as potted plants have attractive foliage year-round. Although some of the plants, such as the *Carex* sp. and *Acorus* sp., grow outdoors in shady locations, this doesn't necessarily mean that they are low light intensity plants under interior conditions. In home conditions, grasses normally require medium to high light intensities and benefit from moist, fertile soil with adequate drainage. A good soil mix is 1 part peat, 1 part vermiculite or perlite, and 1 part sterile soil. A complete fertilizer such as 5-10-10 or 5-10-5 can be mixed into the soil before planting (3 tablespoons per bushel of soil), or one of the slow release fertilizers can be incorporated into the soil mix.

Always use a pot that has adequate drainage, such as a hole in the bottom. Clay or plastic pots which are best for plant growth are not always particularly attractive; these can be placed into larger decorative crocks or colorful pots which completely hide the clay pot.

Water the interior grasses when the top of the soil feels dry to the touch. This may be no more often than once a week or, in bright sunny windows, every 2 or 3 days. Always water until water runs out the bottom of the pot, then drain off this excess water.

After six or eight months, the original soil fertilizer will be depleted and water-soluble solutions (20-20-20 is quite good) should be added every 2 to 4 weeks when the plants are actively growing.

If insects should become troublesome on the leaves, the plants should be sprayed with malathion at the rate of ½ teaspoon per quart of warm water. Two or three applications may be necessary to control the insects, which are usually aphids or white flies. Minor infestations can be controlled by washing the entire plants with soapy lukewarm water solutions.

When the plants become large, check to see if their roots can be seen coming out of the drainage hole in the bottom. If they can, this is a sign that the plant needs to be repotted in a larger container.

5.
Landscape Descriptions
of Ornamental
Grasses

Using the Landscape Descriptions: The landscape descriptions for over ninety grasses are listed in this chapter. They are compiled alphabetically by botanical names. Common names and synonyms are listed in the index.

The descriptions are to provide clear, concise information about the grasses for landscaping as well as for use in decorative arrangements.

Below each botanical name in the descriptions are listed the most important characteristics to be considered before using each plant. These characteristics are followed by a descriptive paragraph.

The key to the characteristics is as follows:

Botanical Name   Common Name
     Height   Duration, Hardiness Zone$_1$ Propagation
Flower Size (length)   Flower Color   Flowering Period$_2$
Foliage Color   Foliage Texture
Plant Form$_3$

1. The winter hardiness rating for each plant is based on hardiness zones recorded by the United States Department of Agriculture, *Plant Hardiness Zone Map*, Misc. Pub. 814, Supt. of DC., Gov. Print. Off., Wash. D.C. See map in the appendix. The zones of hardiness cited for each plant are estimates based on limited research. It is possible that these zones may be revised when more information is known.

Duration refers to annual, perennial, or horticultural annual, terms which are defined in the glossary.

2. Flowering Period—the time in which the flowers and seeds are attractive on the plant.

    1st to 10th day of the month—Early
    11th to 20th day of the month—Mid
    21st to 31st day of the month—Late

e.g. *Pennisetum setaceum* blooms from late July to early Oct. (July 28 to Oct. 8)

3. Plant form for the grasses is divided into seven categories; these are listed in the first section of Chapter 2.

Acorus gramineus "Variegatus"   Japanese Sweet Flag
    8–10″   Perennial, USDA Zone 6   Division
Flowers: 1″   pale green   Sporadic
Foliage: green and white striped   Texture: fine
Plant Form: low, open, and spreading

Japanese Sweet Flag has been a popular interior potted plant for many years. Actually a member of the Arum or Araceae family, it is usually sold in the trade as an ornamental grass. In mild or warm climates it can be grown outdoors in moist or wet soils in full sun or light shade. The fine-textured leaves are striped with white or yellow and remain attractive year-round, either as an interior house plant or an outdoor landscape plant. It grows best in moist or wet soil, and can be used in water or rock gardens or as a specimen plant. Indoors, the plants require medium to high light intensity, and fairly moist soil. Soil mixes of 1 part peat moss, 1 part soil, and 1 part sand are suitable.

The flowers have little value or decorative appeal for dried arrangements.

Agrostis nebulosa   Cloud Grass
   8–24″   Annual   Seed
Flowers: 5–10″   white, pale green   June & July
Foliage: green   Texture: fine
Plant Form: open, spreading

Probably the finest-textured of all grasses, Cloud Grass has minutely branched panicles with very fine slender leaves. The plants can be grown in an annual border, when planted in mass they give a very soft, cloud-like effect. Almost any soil is suitable, although poorly drained sites are not desirable and full sun or light shade produces the best plants.

Unfortunately, Cloud Grass is short-lived and by late summer the plants turn brown. Pick all the flowers; if left in the garden they will self-sow. The flowers are excellent for dried arrangements, resembling a miniature form of Baby's Breath, and dye easily.

Aira capillaris var. *pulchella*   Hair Grass
   8–18″   Annual   Seed
Flowers: 2–5″   white, pale green   Mid-June–Late July
Foliage: green   Texture: fine
Plant Form: open, spreading

Hair Grass is almost identical to Cloud Grass (*Agrostis nebulosa*), but botanically they are in separate genera. Cloud Grass is slightly larger in overall height and flower size. Hair Grass is grown primarily for its delicate flowers to use in dried arrangements. See *Agrostis nebulosa* for site and soil.

Alopecurus pratensis "Aureus"   Meadow Foxtail
   1–3′   Perennial, USDA Zone 5   Division
Flowers: 1–3″   pale green to light yellow   Mid-June–Mid-July
Foliage: yellow and green striped
Plant Form: upright-open

Grown primarily for its striped yellow foliage and clump-forming habit, Meadow Foxtail is suitable for the perennial border, rock garden, or edge of a pool. It prefers fertile, moist soil in full sun or light shade. Native to cool climates, it loses most of its foliage color during the winter. The flowers are insignificant for arrangements; they are short and dense pale yellow spikes. Unfortunately, this variegated form of Foxtail is rarely available in the United States.

Ampelodesmos mauritanicus
   6–12′   Perennial, USDA Zone 8 or 9   Seed, Division
Flowers: 8–20″   light green   Late summer–fall
Foliage: green   Texture: fine
Plant Form: upright-open

Ampelodesmos mauritanicus (unfortunately has no common name) has been grown in the U.S. as a landscape plant only in Southern California. The plants are grown primarily for the flowers that are excellent for arrangements. As evidenced by the plant hardiness zone (above) this grass is not winter hardy in most areas of the U.S. When grown in warm climates, it prefers full sun and moist, fertile soil. During the winter, although the plants cease flowering, they remain semi-ever-green. The flowers are often sold in florist shops and novelty stores and are usually dyed bright colors.

Andropogon scoparius   Little Bluestem
   1½–5′   Perennial, USDA Zone 4   Seed, Division
Flowers: 1–3″   white, light beige   Late July–early winter
Foliage: green, slightly reddish, purple   Texture: fine
Plant Form: upright-open

Little Bluestem is native throughout most of central and eastern U.S. and is often used in soil conservation work to reduce erosion and stabilize roadbanks. Its value as an orna-mental grass lies mostly in its interesting flowers and reddish-brown fall foliage color. Little Bluestem will grow on almost any soil, especially dry or rocky sites, and prefers full sun. It can be used in the garden in naturalized areas or for its cut flowers. The plants remain nearly upright during the winter and the flowers remain attractive on the plant through the fall and winter.

Apera interrupta   Dense Silky Bent Grass
    18–26″   Annual   Seed
Flowers: 2–7″   light green, beige   Late June–Late July
Foliage: green   Texture: fine
Plant Form: upright-open

This annual is grown only for its narrow but thick flowers, which are good for everlasting arrangements. The plants themselves are not an asset in landscaping and they turn brown soon after flowering. Grow the plants in full sun or light shade and provide adequate moisture during the summer. The plants may become prostrate from heavy winds and rain.

Apera spica-venti   Loose Silky Bent Grass
    2–3′   Annual   Seed
Flowers: 8–12″   green, reddish-tan   Mid-June–Late July
Foliage: green
Plant Form: upright-open

This member of the *Apera* genus is by far the more attractive; its flowers are large open panicles which nod softly in the wind. Loose Silky Bent should be grown under the same conditions as Dense Silky Bent.

In the fall, *Apera spica-venti* turns an attractive buff or reddish-tan. It can be grown in the background of an annual border as well as for cut flowers. Both species of *Apera* die with the first fall frost.

Arrhenatherum elatius   Bulbous Oat Grass
Var. *bulbosum* "Variegatum"
   18–25″   Perennial, USDA Zone 5   Division
Flowers: 5–9″   white, yellow, pale green   Early Aug.–
                                                    Late Aug.
Foliage: white & blue-green striped   Texture: fine-medium
Plant Form: upright-open to low-open spreading

The attractive foliage of Bulbous Oat Grass certainly gives it a place among the ornamental grasses. It is a cool season plant and grows best in early spring and fall. Even in cool climates, some of the leaves may turn brown with the heat of midsummer. During the winter, the plants remain slightly evergreen in colder zone (USDA Zone 5) with more color in warmer areas. Because of the bulbous corms, this grass can withstand dry soil or drought conditions and prefers full sun or partial shade.

The flowers are of little value, and the plants are primarily grown for use in the rock garden, perennial border, and as specimen plants.

Arundo donax   Giant Reed
   7–20′   Perennial, USDA Zone 7 or 8   Division, perhaps
                                                    Seed
Flowers: 12–24″   white, light brown   Mid-October–Persist
                                                    into winter
Foliage: light green to blue green   Texture: very coarse
Plant Form: upright-open

The striking foliage, texture, and size of Giant Reed demand special consideration in the landscape (Figure 2). The plants require full sun and well-drained soil with adequate moisture. This plant may require a winter mulch for protection from fluctuating temperatures. When planted in light soils, especially in warm regions, creeping rhizomes may be troublesome.

The flowers are attractive and excellent for drying. They

remain on the plant during winter, thus adding interest in another season of the year.

From an economic standpoint, the tough, hollow stems of *Arundo donax* are valued as a source for reeds for musical instruments.

Arundo donax "Versicolor"   Striped or Variegated Giant Reed
   3–6′   Perennial, USDA Zone 7 or 8   Division
Flowers: 12–24″   white, light green   Mid-Oct.–Persist into
                                         winter
Foliage: green and white striped   Texture: coarse
Plant Form: upright-open

This is one of the tallest variegated grasses; its foliage color and texture make it quite attractive in gardens in warm or mild climates. This variety is not as hardy as the species and requires winter protection in cool climates. Striped Reed can be used in water gardens as a specimen plant or in perennial borders. It is almost identical to the species except for the variegated leaves and shorter height.

Avena fatua   Wild Oat
   2½–3½′   Annual   Seed
Flowers: 7–13″   light green   Late June–Mid-July
Foliage: green   Texture: fine
Plant Form: upright-open

Although Wild Oats is included in this listing of grasses, the plants themselves are far from ornamental and would rarely add to any designed landscape. The flowers, however, are a favorite for dried arrangements and are almost always available from florists or boutiques. The flowering period is short, and at the peak of maturity, the plants rapidly turn brown and die. Thus the decorative heads should be picked early, for if left on the plant, the seeds may readily self-sow.

The flowers are quite attractive when dyed, and although they require a longer period of time in the dye solution, the effort is well worth it.

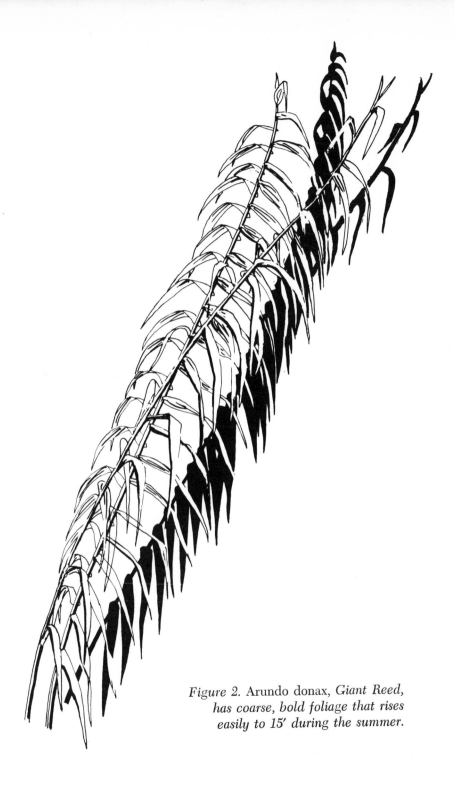

Figure 2. Arundo donax, *Giant Reed,*
has coarse, bold foliage that rises
easily to 15′ during the summer.

Avena sterilis   Animated Oats
   2½–3½′   Annual   Seed
Flowers: 7–13″   light green   Late June–Mid-July
Foliage: green   Texture: medium
Plant Form: upright-open

Animated Oats are very similar to Wild Oats, but are characterized by larger individual flowers with longer awns (hair-like projections up to 1½ inches long) projecting from the flowers. This species is, again, grown only for its decorative flowers which are more desirable than those of Wild Oats. The common name here is derived from the movement of the flowers, which twist and turn (when fresh) according to changes in atmospheric moisture.

Members of the *Avena* genus are ideal for studying the parts of a grass flower, for the flowers are large and easy to see without the aid of a microscope.

Bouteloua gracilis   Side Oats Grama, Mosquito Grass
   8–24″   Perennial USDA, Zone 5   Seed, Division
Flowers: 1–2″   dark purple   Early June–Early Oct.
Foliage: green   Texture: fine
Plant Form: upright-open

This small and unassuming grass needs to be observed at close range to be appreciated. The flowers are quite unusual and are borne on the plant perpendicular to the stem and resemble miniature fine-toothed combs. The overall form adds little to a garden or landscape, except perhaps in a rock garden. The seed can be broadcast over a large area to naturalize, although it may be slow to establish. Side Oats Grama can be grown on dry soils, and it does prefer full sun. The plants have little winter interest although the flowers persist late in the year. The flowers are excellent for dried arrangements, retaining their color and horizontal habit when dried upright, rather

The fall foliage coloration of grasses at the Test Gardens, Cornell University. From left, *Pennisetum alopecuroides*, Fountain Grass; *Miscanthus sacchariflorus*, Eulalia Grass; *Spartina pectinata* 'Aureomarginata,' Cord Grass; and *Elymus arenarius*, Blue Lyme Grass.

Festuca ovina 'Glauca,' Dwarf Blue Fescue, one of the best grasses for ground covers or rock gardens. A variety of mulches can be used with these tufted plants. *Photo by William Frederick.*

One of the oldest ornamental grasses, long considered decorative for its curious bead-like seeds, is *Coix lacryma-jobi,* Job's Tears.

The buff colored plumes of *Erianthus ravennae*, Plume Grass (center), and *Rhus typina*, Staghorn Sumac (right), provide an attractive addition of fall color near a swimming pool.

The annual grasses can make an effective mass planting. Shown here at the L. A. Minns Garden at Cornell University are, from left, buff colored *Apera spica-venti*, Loose Silky Bent Grass; *Lagurus ovatus*, Hare's-tail Grass; *Pennisetum setaceum*, Fountain Grass; *Eragrostis trichodes*, Love Grass (foreground); *Coix lacryma-jobi*, Job's Tears (upper right); *Stipa arundinacea*, orange foliage (lower right); and *Festuca ovina* var. *duriuscula*, Hard Fescue.

Miscanthus sinensis, Japanese Silver Grass, can make an effective screen. This photo was taken before it flowered. At left is Rudbeckia.

Annual border of grasses spaced 6–12″ apart, depending upon their height. In the foreground, *Polypogon monsoeliensis,* Rabbit's-foot Grass; midground from left, *Apera spica-venti,* Loose Silky Bent Grass, *Festuca ovina* var. *duriuscula,* Hard Fescue; *Lagurus ovatus,* Hare's-tail Grass; background, *Coix lacryma-jobi,* Job's Tears.

Rudbeckia, or Black-eyed Susan, is just one of the many flowering perennials that complement the grasses in a perennial border. Shown also is *Pennisetum alopecuroides*, Fountain Grass. *Photo by William Frederick.*

The dense furry flowers of Hare's-tail Grass, *Lagurus ovatus*, are ideal for drying. They are often dyed bright colors and sold in florist and novelty shops.

A collection of the many grasses that are suitable for dyeing. These bright colors are best achieved by placing the flowers in a hot water dye solution.

than hung upside down. There is no need to dye them for they are dark purple or red.

Briza maxima   Puffed Wheat, Large Quaking Grass
    1–2′   Annual   Seed
Flowers: 2–4″   long white, light green   Mid-June–Late July
each floret ½–⅞″
Foliage: green   Texture: medium
Plant Form: upright-open

    This is a typical annual ornamental grass which has decorative flowers but is a rather uninteresting and undesirable overall plant form for use in the landscape. When grown for cut flowers, the plants should be placed in full sun in the cut flower or vegetable garden, and not in a prominent landscape position.
    The flowers are very light, puffy florets that nod and quake in the slightest breeze. The flowers are excellent for drying and dyeing. This is one of the oldest genera of ornamental grasses; it is mentioned in some of the first herbals or plant books ever written.

Briza media   Quaking Grass*
    20–32″   Perennial, USDA Zone 5   Seed, Division
Flowers: 2–4″,   beige, lt. green   Late June–Late July
each floret ½–¼″ long
Foliage: green   Texture: medium
Plant Form: upright-open

    This is the perennial form of Quaking Grass; its flowers are medium-sized and excellent for drying and dyeing. The overall form of the plants is not of great interest; the leaves are tufted near the base and the flower stalks rise about 2 feet above the leaves. Plant in full sun and well-drained soil. The flowers are quite firm and can be picked anytime during flowering or later in the year. Occasionally, fungus diseases may cause orange or yellow spots on the leaves; the best control is an application of one of the fungicides recommended for turf grasses diseases.

* Other common names include Trembling Grass, Doddering Grass, Rattle, Lady's Hair Grass, Dider, Pearl, and Quakers.

Briza minor   Little Quaking Grass
    6–18″   Annual   Seed
Flowers: 2–4″,   lt. green   Mid-June–Early July
each floret ⅛″ long
Plant Form: upright-open

This grass, as the common name implies, is the miniature form of Quaking Grass. Like *B. maxima,* this is also a short-lived annual, with value for cut flowers but hardly any interest as a permanent or even summer landscape plant. Little Quaking Grass grows best in full sun with fertile soil. The plants are not drought tolerant and once the seed is formed, a hot, dry period will cause the entire plant to rapidly turn brown and die. Little Quaking Grass is also subject to damage from heavy wind and rain, which flatten the plants.

Bromus macrostachys   Brome Grass
    1–2′   Annual   Seed
Flowers: 4–7″   lt. green, beige   Mid-June–Mid-August
Foliage: green   Texture: fine
Plant Form: open and spreading

This particular species of Brome Grass is just one of many which are available in the trade. The Brome Grasses are excellent for dried arrangements, and although the flowers may be difficult to dye, they are worth the effort.

The plants need full sun and adequate moisture throughout the growing season, and have no use or interest except for the cut flowers.

Bromus brizaeformis, Bromus catharticus, Bromus inermis,

Bromus japonicus, Bromus madritensis, and *Bromus mollis* are some of the other species grown for their decorative flowers.

Calamagrostis epigeous   Reed Grass
   3–6′   Perennial, USDA Zone 5   Division, Seed
Flowers: 10–24″   green–dk. purple   Late June–Late July
Foliage: green   Texture: medium
Plant Form: upright-open

   Reed Grass is usually grown for its decorative flowers and slender upright habit of growth. It is a favorite plant for water gardens and near ponds, for it tolerates a high moisture content in the soil. It can also be grown in perennial borders or perhaps as a specimen plant. The flowers are dense panicles which spread open with age, excellent for dried arrangements. The plants are not evergreen, but there is some interest in the flowers in winter, for they persist on the plant. Reed Grass is native to sandy soils, and near fresh as well as salt water marshes, ponds, and streams. In light soils it can become invasive due to creeping rhizomes, but in heavy clay soils these are usually confined and not a problem.

Carex buchananii   Leatherleaf Sedge Grass
   1–2′   Hort. Annual USDA Zone 5   Division
           Perennial, USDA Zone 6
Flowers: 1–2″   beige, light brown   Sporadic
Foliage: reddish or coppery-brown   Texture: fine
Plant Form: upright-arching

   This unique grass (really a sedge) is grown for the reddish-brown foliage that is borne on the plant year-round. The leaves are very narrow ($\frac{1}{16}$–$\frac{1}{8}$″) with long curled tips. The flowers are insignificant and the plants are grown for use in water gardens, as specimen plants, or in the midground of a perennial border. Full sun or partial shade with moist soil produces the best plants. This sedge may be slow to become established after transplanting.

Figure 3. Carex morrowii 'Variegata' is one of the smallest grasses. It is ideal for a rock garden, border or edging plant, or as a potted interior plant. The striped foliage is evergreen or semi-evergreen in warm climates or when grown indoors.

Carex morrowii "Variegata"   Japanese Sedge Grass
     6–12"   Perennial, USDA Zone 6   Division
Flowers: 1–2"   green   Sporadic
Foliage: yellow, green, and white striped   Texture: fine
Plant Form: low, mound

    The decorative foliage of Japanese Sedge Grass is attractive year-round. The leaves usually arch around the base of the plant forming a low mound of yellow, green, and white striped leaves. This plant performs well as an interior potted plant if grown in adequate light and with a moist ($1/3$–$1/2$ peat moss) soil mix. When grown outdoors, choose a moist soil location with some shade (may be grown in full sun in cooler climates). Japanese Sedge Grass is not winter hardy as far north as USDA Zone 5, but in milder climates it can be used as a specimen plant, in the foreground of a perennial border, in the rock garden, or near water. Primarily grown for its attractive foliage and low plant form (figure 3).

Carex pendula   Pendulous Sedge Grass
       2–3½′   Perennial, USDA Zone 5   Division
Flowers: 2–4″   brown   Early June–Mid-August
Foliage: dark green   Texture: medium
Plant Form: mound to upright arching

Pendulous Sedge Grass is grown for its evergreen (semi-evergreen in Zone 5) foliage which provides a mound of rich green color in the garden. The plants should be grown in at least partial if not heavy shade with moist soil. The perennial border water garden and locations requiring a specimen plant are good settings for *Carex pendula*. In dividing older plants, keep in mind that smaller divisions are slow to become established.

Carex pendula, Pendulous Sedge Grass, is grown for its rich green foliage that blends well with other evergreens.

Carex riparia "Variegata"   Pond Sedge
    1–2½′   Perennial, USDA Zone 5   Division
Flowers: 1–2″   green, white   Sporadic
Foliage: green with slender white stripes   Texture: fine–medium
Plant Form: mound

Another sedge which is grown for its decorative foliage, this
one with predominantly green leaves with narrow white or
yellow stripes. Although some sources list this plant as nearly
5 feet tall, it is more often seen as a small plant suited for the
perennial border, rock garden, water garden, as a specimen
plant, or as an interior potted plant. Like all sedges, moist
soils with light sun are the best for healthy plant growth.
Pond Sedge has interest year-round for its foliage is evergreen,
even in USDA Zone 5.

Coix lacryma-jobi   Job's Tears
    3–4′   Annual   Seed
Flowers: 3–4″   gray-black;   green   Mid-June–Late Sept.
Foliage: green to yellow green   Texture: coarse
Plant Form: upright-open, upright-narrow

One of the first grasses (in early herbals) considered to be
ornamental, more or less from a curiosity aspect, was Job's
Tears. However, the coarse leaves and stiff upright growth are
somewhat questionable ornamental characteristics for garden
use. The seeds (½ inch long) are dark gray or black when
mature on the plant and make quite a contrast in color next
to the green leaves. These dark seeds are the pistillate or
female flowers, above which are borne the green nodding
staminate or male flowers. The seeds can be collected when
fully mature (they will readily fall from the plant at maturity)
and used to make jewelry; in the Orient, they were ground
into flour.

Job's Tears can be grown in full sun, although larger plants
are produced in partial shade with moist or even wet soil.

In East Asia, where the plants are native, they grow as perennials, but in the U.S. the plants are usually annuals.

To hasten germination, soak the seeds in water for 24 hours before planting. If the seeds are allowed to develop and fall in the garden, they usually self-sow.

Cortaderia selloana   Pampas Grass
     3–20'   Hort. Annual USDA Zone 5–7   Division, Seed
               Perennial USDA Zone 8
Flowers: 20–36″   white, pale pink   Late Sept.–Late Oct.
Foliage: green   Texture: fine to medium
Plant Form: upright-open to upright-narrow

Often called the Queen of the Ornamental Grasses because

Pampas Grass, Cortaderia selloana, *shown here in a desert setting, is known as the "Queen of the Ornamental Grasses" due to its stately flowers and large overall form.* Photo by George Taloumis.

of its large stately appearance, Pampas Grass is a striking
garden plant. It is the tallest decorative grass, but it has limited use in the northern United States because it is question-
ably winter hardy below 20°F. Many of the older gardening
books suggest digging the roots of Pampas Grass in the fall
and placing them in a cellar or basement to keep them over
the winter.

The plants grow best in full sun and fertile soil, although
plantings in dry soil locations may do well.

The large flowers are excellent for dried arrangements and
often remain on the plants in late fall and winter. Because of
the striking appearance of Pampas Grass, it should be located
in the garden where it will not detract from the overall appearance of the garden.

The plants of *Cortaderia* are dioecious, that is, the male
and female flowers are borne on different plants. The female
flowers are the showiest, because of the hairs covering the tiny
flowers. In purchasing or dividing plants, care should be taken
to obtain female plants.

There are reported to be many ornamental forms of Pampas
Grass. Some have pink or purple flowers, and others are
smaller plants that only reach 4 to 5 feet tall. The variety
Cortaderia selloana "Pumila" is often listed as the dwarf form.
Cortaderia Richardii flowers in early August with 8 to 15 inch
plumes that are pale yellow; the plants are 6 to 7 feet tall.
Unfortunately, very few, if any, of these different forms are
sold in the U.S.

Cymbopogon citratus   Lemon Grass
   1–6′   Perennial USDA Zone 10
Flowers: sporadic and not conspicuous
Foliage: light green–yellow–green
Plant Form: Upright-arching to irregular

Although this grass has an attractive overall form with
upright arching leaves, it is not a winter hardy species for

the majority of the U.S. In tropical climates, at maturity it may be as tall as 6 feet. It is doubtful if it would tolerate winter temperature below 40°F.

Lemon Grass can be grown as a potted plant for herb or fragrance gardens, for its leaves, when crushed, have a delightful lemon fragrance. This plant is the commercial source of lemon oil.

Dactylis glomerata "Variegata"   Striped Cock's-foot Grass
Striped Orchard Grass
1–2½′   Perennial USDA Zone 5   Division
Flowers: 1–2″   light green   Mid-June–Late July
Foliage: green and white striped   Texture: fine
Plant Form: open and spreading to mound

This is a striped form of the common weed Orchard Grass. The foliage color is decorative during spring and summer, but turns brown in late fall. The flowers are of little ornamental value, and usually this species is grown for rock gardens, as a ground cover for a small area, or as a specimen plant.

Locations of full sun or partial shade are ideal. This species is rarely found in the trade in the United States.

Deschampsia caespitosa   Tufted Hair Grass
20–36″   Perennial USDA Zone 5   Division, Seed
Flowers: 10–15″   white, light green   Late June–Late Aug.
Foliage: dark to medium green   Texture: fine to medium
Plant Form: mound

This densely tufted grass is grown for its overall attractive form and mass of early blooming flowers. The plants will grow on moist soils, or in dry locations of full sun or partial to full shade. The plants may remain somewhat green in winter, but are of little interest at this time.

The flowers are open, slightly nodding, feathery panicles that are excellent for dried arrangements. In landscaping, Tufted Hair Grass can be used in perennial borders, the rock garden, water gardens, or in naturalized areas. The long flowering period assures interest in the plants all summer long.

A variant of this species exists in which the flowers are replaced by small purple-green bulblets, and the total flower is coarser and heavier.

Deschampsia flexuosa   Wavy Hair Grass
    8″–2½′   Perennial USDA Zone 5
Flowers: 2–5″   lt. green, lt. brown   Late June–Late July
Foliage: green   Texture: very fine
Plant Form: tufted to upright-open

This delicate grass is grown for its overall form and decorative flowers. The leaves are tufted at the base of the plant and the panicles rise far along the leaves on narrow, somewhat wiry stems.

Moist or dry locations in full sun or partial to full shade are suitable. In addition to drying the flowers for arrangements, the plants can be grown for rock gardens, in the foreground of perennial borders, or in naturalized areas.

Even though the leaves are semi-evergreen, they create little attractive interest for the winter.

Desmazeria sicula   Spike Grass
    8–12″   Annual   Seed
Flowers: 1–3″   beige, light green   Late June–Early Aug.
Foliage: green   Texture: medium
Plant Form: open and spreading

This low-growing annual is similar to the *Briza* species in cultivation and value as an ornamental. The flowers are the only reason for growing the plants in a garden. The attractive panicles can be cut and are excellent for dried arrangements. Because the plants are annuals and their overall form is not desirable in the formal garden, they are best grown in the cut flower or vegetable garden. Plant the seed directly outside in early spring in full sun and well-drained soil.

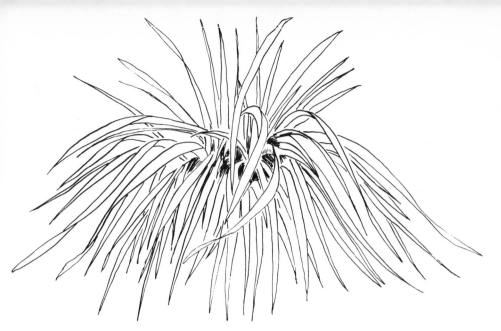

Figure 4. Blue Lyme Grass, Elymus arenarius, *has a unique blue foliage color that will complement any perennial border.*

Elymus arenarius   Blue Wild Rye, Blue Lyme Grass
   2–4′   Perennial USDA Zone 4   Division
Flowers: 6–12″   beige, light blue-green   Late June–Early Aug.
Foliage: light blue   Texture: coarse
Plant Form: irregular

This is the largest ornamental grass with light blue foliage (figure 4). Blue Lyme Grass is grown primarily for its foliage color; its flowers are beige spikes which may rarely appear on the plants.

Locations of full sun with moist, wet, or dry soils are suitable for this species. It is especially well-suited for use in a perennial border where the light blue foliage can be contrasted with bright flower colors. It may also be grown as a specimen plant or in water gardens.

Blue Lyme Grass has stout creeping rhizomes that can only be kept in place by heavy clay soils or by bottomless containers sunk into the ground around the roots. In gardens this is a distinct disadvantage, but on seashores or in conservation planting, these rhizomes are often valued as a means of soil stabilization.

Elymus glaucus is a very similar species; the only difference is that this type does not have creeping rhizomes. Unfortunately, *Elymus glaucus* is rarely available in the trade.

The flowers of both species are not of particular ornamental value. *Elymus arenarius* flowers sporadically and may grow for several years before flowering.

Elymus interruptus   Nodding Lyme Grass
   3–5′   Perennial USDA Zone 5   Seed, Division
Flowers: 5–10″   light brown   Late July–Persist into winter
Foliage: green   Texture: coarse
Plant Form: upright-open

This large, rather coarse-textured grass is grown primarily for its long spikes of nodding flowers which are interesting on the plant as well as in dried arrangements. The plants themselves are not particularly attractive, and although they are perennial, they rarely deserve a prominent garden position.

Locate the plants in full sun or light shade in dry or moist soils.

As the plants become older, they form rhizomes and may spread slowly; usually heavy clay soils are sufficient to keep the roots in bounds.

Eragrostis curvula   Weeping Love Grass
   3–5′   Perennial USDA Zone 5   Division, Seed
Flowers: 10–15″   dark gray-green   Late June–Early Aug.
Foliage: green   Texture: fine
Plant Form: upright-open to upright-arching

A fine arching mound of leaves topped with long nodding flowers gives Weeping Love Grass an attractive overall form. The flowers are dark gray-green and can be used for dried arrangements. The plants are attractive through summer and early fall, until hard freezes turn the entire plant pale beige.

Figure 5. *Weeping Love Grass is one of the perennial species in the Eragrostis genus. The flowers of this genus are very narrow when first borne on the plant and become open and wide-spreading as they mature.*

In locations of full sun with well-drained soil, the plants grow best. The flowers are light and easily knocked over by heavy winds and rain. If the panicles are not all picked by maturity, the seeds may drop and the plants self-sow quite easily.

In landscaping, the plants can be grown in the perennial border or in naturalized areas (Figure 5).

Eragrostis trichodes   Sand Love Grass
   2–3½'   Perennial USDA Zone 5   Seed, Division
Flowers: 9–20"   light green   Early–Late Aug.
Foliage: light green   Texture: medium
Plant Form: upright-arching

This is one of the many species of Love Grass that is grown for its long wide spreading flowers and open-arching plant form.

The plants should be grown in full sun, with adequate moisture. In landscaping, placement may be in a perennial border or in naturalized areas.

The flowers of Love Grass are long, arching, narrow panicles when they are first borne on the plant. With age, these narrow panicles spread wide open–up to 1 foot wide. If picked young and dried upright, they can be used to provide line and form to arrangements. The young narrow flowers resemble fine sprays of Scotch Broom.

Some of the other species also grown for ornamental purposes are: *Eragrostis tef, Eragrostis capillaris,* and *Eragrostis abyssinica.*

Erianthus ravennae   Plume Grass
   7–15'   Perennial USDA Zone 5   Division
Flowers: 12–20"   silvery white, beige   Late Sept.–Late Oct.
Foliage: green   Texture: coarse
Plant Form: upright-open

Plume Grass is by far one of the loveliest ornamental grasses due to its flowers and striking overall form. This is the tallest

Figure 6. Plume Grass is one of the best flowers for dried arrangements. This is also the hardiest large grass and can be grown as far north as central New York.

ornamental grass that is winter hardy as far north as USDA Zone 5.

In full sun, with fertile, well-drained soil, the plants can easily reach 10 to 12 feet, even in the Northeast.

The flowers are borne in late fall, and remain attractive on the plant until late winter. In October, as cool weather comes, the plants turn an attractive brown fall color, tinged with orange and purple. During winter the brown color persists.

In addition to using the flowers for dried arrangements, the plants are excellent for landscaping water gardens, perennial borders, or for use as specimen plants or as screens.

In cold climates, early fall frosts may interfere with flowering. In warmer climates, flowers should not be allowed to go to seed, as the plants self-sow readily.

Festuca amethystina   Large Blue Fescue
    1½–3′   Perennial USDA Zone 5   Division, Seed
Flowers: 1–2″   light brown, green   Mid-June–Mid-July
Foliage: blue to blue-green   Texture: fine
Plant Form: tufted

Although the height of this plant is listed as up to 3 feet, the leaves are usually tufted and basal, with the flower stalks rising far above the leaves. The dense, tufted, light blue foliage make this Fescue a welcome addition to the foreground of a perennial border, in the rock garden, as a ground cover, or as a specimen plant.

The plants grow best in full sun to light shade and although well-drained soils are a *requirement* for most Fescues, this species is more tolerant of wet soils than most. In warmer climates this type is often grown rather than *Festuca ovina* "Glauca."

The flowers are not of ornamental value.

Festuca gigantea   Giant Fescue

1½–5′   Perennial USDA Zone 5   Seed, Division
Flowers: 4–8″   light green   Mid-July–Late August
Foliage: bright green   Texture: medium
Plant Form: upright-open to upright-arching

This is the largest Fescue grown as an ornamental. In gardens, it is used primarily for its bright shiny green foliage, which grows easily in the full sun or light to full shade in many soil sites. It may be placed in the perennial border in the midground or in naturalized areas.

The foliage is semi-evergreen during the winter, but the major interest is in the summer.

The flowers are of little value for arrangements.

Festuca ovina "Glauca"   Dwarf Blue Fescue

6–12″   Perennial, USDA Zone 4   Division
Flowers: 1–2″   green, beige   Early June–Early July
Foliage: silvery blue to light blue   Texture: fine
Plant Form: tufted

This is probably the most attractive and widely used dwarf ornamental grass. Dwarf Blue Fescue has long been valued for its light, silvery-blue foliage which retains its color year-round. The plants prefer cool climates (north of Philadelphia, Pa.) in full sun to light shade and require well-drained soils for success. Rocky, dry soils on slopes are preferable to flat

Figure 7. The dense blue tufts of Festuca ovina *'Glauca,' Blue Fescue, are good for year-round color in the garden. Well-drained soil is the only requirement for this species.*

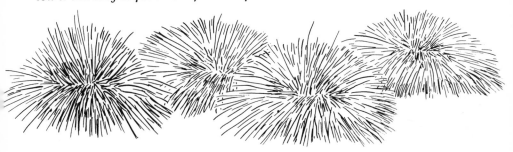

areas where water may collect. In such heavy clay soils, the plants will be short-lived and tend to die in the center, thus requiring more frequent division.

In landscaping, the plants are excellent for specimens, in the foreground of a perennial border, in rock gardens, or as a ground cover (Figure 7).

The flowers have no ornamental value.

The foliage color of Dwarf Blue Fescue may vary widely. Variants are available which range from yellow-green to various shades of blue-green.

Festuca ovina var. *duriuscula*   Hard Fescue
    6–10″   Perennial USDA Zone 5   Division, Seed
Flowers: 1–2″   light green   Early June–Early July
Foliage: blue-green, glaucous   Texture: fine
Plant Form: tufted

The broad foliage of Hollyhocks, upper left, and fine texture of primroses, lower left, contrast with tufted Festuca ovina *var.* duriuscula, *Hard Fescue.*

This variety may often be sold in the trade as *Festuca ovina* "Glauca," but Hard Fescue can be distinguished by its wider (1⁄16–1⁄8" wide), firmer leaves, and usually darker gray-blue color.

See *Festuca ovina* "Glauca" for site selection and landscape uses, for the two can be used identically in the garden.

Glyceria maxima "Variegata"   Sweet or Manna Grass
    1½–3'   Perennial USDA Zone 5   Division
Flowers: 6–12"   light green-yellow   Mid-July–Mid-Aug.
Foliage: green, white, and yellow striped   Texture: medium-
                                                                                coarse
Plant Form: irregular

This striped grass is quite popular for use at the edge of ponds and streams. This is one of the few ornamental plants that can be grown *in* the water, not just at the edge of water. Place either in full sun or light shade.

The plants turn brown during the winter and are of little interest at this time.

In light sandy soils, they may spread by creeping rhizomes; the plants are best confined heavy clay soils or by containers sunken in the grounds around the roots.

The flowers are of little ornamental value. This species may be difficult to find in the U.S. trade.

Helictotrichon sempervirens   Blue Oat Grass
    2–3', 4' with flowers   Perennial USDA Zone 5   Division
Flowers: 3–4"   beige   Early June–Early July
Foliage: light glaucous blue   Texture: fine to medium
Plant Form: tufted

Blue Oat Grass is a large tufted grass, grown primarily for its light blue foliage. Its overall form resembles a Yucca (without the flowers), but the texture is much finer and, of course, the foliage is blue (Figure 8).

This species prefers full sun, and it is tolerant of a wide

variety of soils. In landscaping, the plants can be used in the perennial border, as a specimen plant, or in the rock garden.

The plants are semi-evergreen during the winter. In shady locations, they may become weak and open; excessive humidity or moist conditions may promote leaf spot diseases.

The flowers are of little value for arrangements; they are conspicuous when borne on the plants for they rise far above the leaves and are white or light beige.

Holcus mollis "Variegatus"   Velvet Grass
     4–12″   Perennial, USDA Zone 5   Division
Flowers: 1–2″   green and white   Early June and Early Aug.
Foliage: green and white striped   Texture: fine to medium
Plant Form: low, open, and spreading

Figure 8. A different plant for the foreground of a border is Blue Oat Grass, Helictotrichon sempervirens. Its common name is derived from the flowers that are borne only on mature specimens and slightly resemble the common cereal grass.

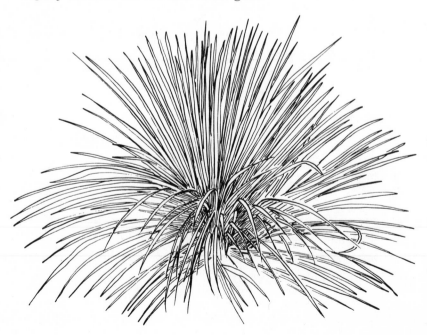

Three are two species of Velvet Grass, *Holcus mollis* and *Holcus lanatus*, which have variegated or striped forms that are grown as ornamentals. The striped form of *Holcus lanatus* is, however, more desirable, because it forms a tufted grass, rather than a creeping form like *Holcus mollis*, which has underground rhizomes. Both are short, dainty grasses which are suitable for use in the foreground of perennial borders, in rock gardens, as ground covers, or as specimen plants.

Sites of full sun or light shade with well-drained soils are best. These species are semi- or totally "evergreen," or they retain their striped foliage year-round.

The flowers are not ornamental and often look unattractive on the plants because they detract from the foliage. The flowers can be clipped off as they form. When using *Holcus mollis*, remember that its roots will need confining to keep them from becoming a nuisance.

Hordeum jubatum   Foxtail Barley, Squirrel's-tail Grass
     20–30″   Perennial, Biennial USDA Zone 5   Seed
Flowers: 3–4″   dark red, purple, or green   Early June–
                                                 Early July
Foliage: green   Texture: fine to medium
Plant Form: upright-open

Hordeum jubatum is one of the earliest grasses to flower in the spring, and it is very showy when in flower, for the whole plant becomes a mass of silky, nodding blooms.

It grows best in full sun and either moist or dry soils. In landscaping this species can be used in the perennial border or in naturalized areas. After flowering, it has no interest in late summer, fall, or winter.

The plants are very light and open; they can easily be knocked down from winds and rain.

These flowers readily fall apart at maturity and the plants can become a nuisance because they self-sow easily. The flowers are attractive for fresh or dried arrangements, but as dried flowers they often shatter with age. The long awns or hairs in each tiny flower may be injurious to animals because these enable the seed to adhere to their fur and burrow in their hide.

Hordeum vulgare   Barley
   2–4′   Annual   Seed
Flowers: 1–4″   beige   Mid-July–Late Aug.
Foliage: green   Texture: medium
Plant Form: upright-narrow

This is the common form of cultivated barley, included here only for its value as a dried flower for arrangements. The plants have no value for landscape use and the flowering period is short, after which the plants turn totally brown.

Barley and wheat (*Triticum* sp.) are often used in florist shops for arrangements and natural bouquets.

Barley can be differentiated from wheat by the number of spikelets or small florets grouped together along the flowering stem. Barley has three fattened spikelets (or seeds) grouped together while wheat has only one spikelet, or seed, at each joint along the flowering stem. Both of these grasses usually have long, hair-like projections or awns extending from the spikelets or flowers.

Hystrix patula   Bottlebrush Grass
   2–4′   Perennial, USDA Zone 5   Seed, Division
Flowers: 5–8″   light green   Early July–Mid-Oct.
Foliage: green   Texture: medium
Plant Form: upright-open

This is one of the best-suited grasses for shady sites in moist or dry soil. It can be grown in full sun, but in such a location the plants may be shorter or form yellowish leaves. The in-

Figure 9. It's easy to see how Hystrix patula, *Bottlebrush Grass, got its common name. A valuable plant for shady, moist locations, it is a hardy perennial.*

dividual plants have an attractive upright open form and with the flowers, the plants are useful in the midground of the perennial border, in water gardens, or for naturalized areas.

The flowers are quite stiff and indeed resemble bottle brushes, hence the common name. In dried arrangements the flowers are quite useful, especially if cut early. They are difficult to dye successfully because of their tough, dry flowers.

Native to the Eastern United States, this grass is often seen in woodlands and moist, shady locations.

Imperata sp.   Satintail
  2–3½′   Perennial, USDA Zone 8 or 9   Seed, Division
Flowers: 4–12″   silvery white   Late July–Late Aug.
Foliage: green   Texture: medium to fine
Plant Form: upright-open

Satintail is rarely grown in gardens but it is a popular dried grass for arrangements. The plants have little landscape value, except for the silvery flowers borne in late summer. The scaly rhizomes are quite vigorous and can cause the plants to be invasive. Locations in full sun with almost any soil type are suitable.

The flowers are soft and silky; their natural color is white to silver. Satintail is one of the easiest flowers to dye; the colors come through consistently and bright. The later the flowers are picked, the more they will shatter as they mature.

Koeleria cristata "Glauca"   Blue June Grass
  6–18″   Perennial, USDA Zone 5   Division
Flowers: 2–4″   silvery white   Mid-June–Mid-July
Foliage: blue-green   Texture: fine
Plant Form: upright-open

The genus *Koeleria* contains only a few species grown in the United States. *Koeleria cristata* is a good forage plant and grows throughout much of the western United States. The variant "Glauca" is a low-growing tufted plant with blue-green foliage. Often this is listed in the trade as *Koeleria glauca,* but most plants available in the U.S. are variants of the *Koeleria cristata* species.

Blue June Grass is grown primarily for its evergreen to semi-evergreen foliage color and overall plant height. It can be used in rock gardens or in the foreground of perennial borders. The plants prefer full sun or partial shade. Although the flowers are attractive in mass on the plant, they have little value for dried arrangements.

Lagurus ovatus   Hare's-tail Grass
    10–20″   Annual   Seed
Flowers: ¾–2″   light green   Early June–Early Aug.
Foliage: light green   Texture: fine to medium
Plant Form: upright-open to irregular

This is propably the most popular annual grass grown for use in dried arrangements. Hare's-tail Grass is excellent for cutting and drying because the flowers stay intact and are easily handled without shattering.

The plants can be grown in mass for the annual or perennial flower border, they flower profusely, but are dying by early August. Full sun or light shade with adequate moisture produces the most flowers.

Hare's-tail is easy to grow from seed sown directly in the garden or from plants started indoors in early spring. The flowers are fairly easy to dye.

Lamarkia aurea   Golden Top
    6–18″   Annual   Seed
Flowers: 2–4″   yellow to light green   Late June–Early Aug.
Foliage: green   Texture: fine
Plant Form: open and spreading

This is one of the more colorful flowering annual grasses due to the yellow-green flowers. Other than the flowers, the plants have little or no landscape value.

Lagurus ovatus, *Hare's-tail Grass, is one of the most decorative annual grasses. Its flowers are numerous and dry so easily that it deserves a place in any cut flower garden.*

The seed of Golden Top may be difficult to germinate; many of the florets are sterile, so a larger percentage of seed should be sown. The plants can be sown directly outdoors or the seed can be started indoors in early spring. Place the plants outdoors in full sun or light shade in locations with adequate soil moisture.

The flowers, although quite attractive when borne on the plants, often shatter when cut and dried, and their color fades slightly when dry.

Luzula sp.   White Woodrush
    18–24″   Perennial, USDA Zone 5   Division
Flowers: 2–5″   white, ivory   Early June–Mid-July
Foliage: green   Texture: fine to medium
Plant Form: upright-arching

The White Woodrush that is available and sold in the trade in the United States has rather large clusters of white or slightly ivory flowers. Most of these specimens do not fit the description of *Luzula sylvatica* or *Luzula nivea*, even though this is how they are listed in the trade. Despite the confusion over nomenclature, the two species just mentioned, as well as those sold in the U.S., are all members of the Woodrush family and are decorative additions to the garden. They flower quite early and are grown for their flowers as well as overall plant form. The plants are semi-evergreen and suited for shady locations in moist soil in the perennial border, water gardens, naturalized areas, and in rock gardens.

The foliage is an attractive green and, like most woodrushes, there are conspicuous white hairs at the leaf margins.

The flowers are excellent for dried bouquets and can be dyed fairly easily.

Melica altissima "Atropurpurea"   Melic Grass
    2–3½′   Perennial, USDA Zone 5   Division
Flowers: 3–6″   deep purple   Late June–Late July
Foliage: green   Texture: fine to medium
Plant Form: upright-open

Unfortunately, this variety is rarely available in the United States. It is a form grown primarily for its dark purple flowers.

The plants can be grown in locations of full sun or partial shade in moist soil. They have little interest except during flowering when they are attractive in perennial borders or naturalized areas.

The flowers can be dried and used for bouquets; they fade somewhat, but do not shatter readily.

Millium effusum "Aureum"   Millet Grass
    1½–2½′   Perennial, USDA Zone 6   Division
Flowers: 4–8″   yellow, light green   Mid-June–Mid-July
Foliage: light green-yellow   Texture: fine-medium
Plant Form: upright-open

This is another colorful grass that is rarely available in the United States. The species *Millium effusum* is a woodland perennial in the northeastern U.S. This form is grown, however, for its yellow flowers and foliage that are especially showy in the spring. It is quite tolerant of partial or full shade and does best in moist fertile soil. The plants can be grown in perennial borders, water gardens, or as a ground cover.

The flowers can be cut for bouquets and are quite attractive in dried arrangements. If the flowers are left in the garden, the plants reseed themselves quite easily.

Miscanthus sacchariflorus   Eulalia Grass
    5–10′   Perennial, USDA Zone 5   Division, Seed
Flowers: 7–10″   silvery white   Early Aug.–Persist into winter
Foliage: green   Texture: medium to coarse
Plant Form: upright-narrow to upright open

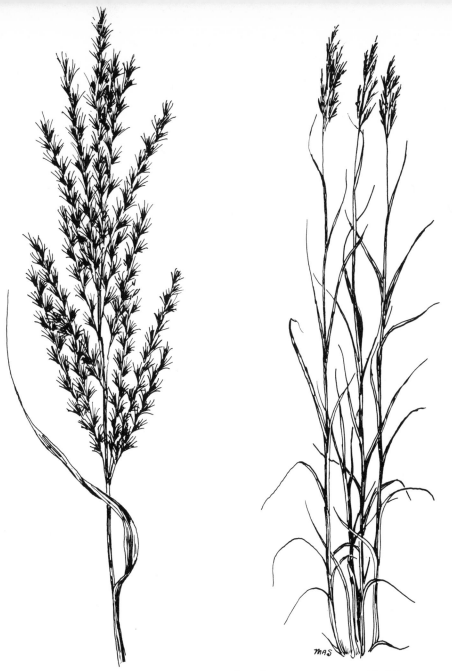

Figure 10. Miscanthus sacchariflorus *has the common name Eulalia Grass, which is almost as difficult to pronounce as the botanical name. Nevertheless, the flowers are graceful and fluffy white in fall and winter and are a welcome sight at this time in the garden.*

This is one of two species of *Miscanthus*, a large and popular group of ornamental grasses. The species *Miscanthus sacchariflorus* is characterized by creeping rhizomes, especially troublesome in warm climates; white, silvery flowers, rather than reddish-pink flowers; and although the individual flowers are surrounded by soft, numerous hairs, the solitary stiff, coarse awn, or hair-like projection from the back of the floret, is absent in *Miscanthus sacchariflorus* and present in *Miscanthus sinensis*.

This is one of the taller grasses; its flowers are very attractive in the fall and add interest as they persist on the plant all winter. In fall, the foliage turns a rather bright orange and remains light orange through the winter.

The leaves at the bottom of the plant usually turn brown and are unattractive during the summer. For this reason, the plants are best used in the background of a perennial border (Figure 10).

Full sun is the only requirement for *Miscanthus* and this particular species can also be grown in the water garden, naturalized areas, or as a screen.

The flowers are one of the best for drying and dyeing. If left to go to seed in warm climates, this species often self-sows and can be troublesome. The rhizomes are not troublesome if planted in heavy clay soils or if the roots are confined in light soils.

Miscanthus sacchariflorus "Giganteus"   Giant Eulalia,
                                           Giant Miscanthus
    9–16′   Perennial, USDA Zone 7 or 8   Division
Flowers: 7–10″   silvery white   Mid-Oct.–Persist to winter
Foliage: green   Texture: coarse
Plant Form: upright-narrow

This form of *Miscanthus*, although without creeping rhizomes, still has no awn, or stiff, coarse, hair-like projection from the back of the individual flower, and thus is considered *Miscanthus sacchariflorus*, not *Miscanthus sinensis*.

This variant is truly a giant, due to its large size and coarse texture. It grows very quickly during the first few months of the growing season and makes an excellent screen. The plants require full sun and warm, or at least mild climatic conditions. The plants are large and thus more difficult to place in the landscape, but they could be useful additions to the perennial border or water garden (near formal or informal pools).

The flowers are excellent for drying and dyeing.

Miscanthus sinensis   Eulalia Grass, Japanese Silver Grass
    7–13′   Perennial, USDA Zone 4   Division
Flowers: 7–10″   pale pink or red   Mid-Sept.–Persist into
                                          winter

Foliage: green   Texture: medium
Plant Form: upright-open

This is one of the most popular ornamental grasses, grown for its flowers as well as overall plant form. This species is clump-forming; it does not have creeping rhizomes. Even when mature, the plants are not extremely large or difficult to place in landscapes. Perennial borders, water gardens, and naturalized areas are suitable locations for Japanese Silver Grass. It can also be grown as a specimen plant or screen. Full sun is the only requirement for location and many soil types are suitable. If grown in shady locations or very fertile soil, the plants may require staking. Although the plants turn brown during the winter, the flowers remain attractive until early spring.

The flowers are among the best for drying and dyeing.

Miscanthus sinensis "Gracillimus"   Maiden Grass
Flowers: 7–10″   silvery white   Mid-Oct.–Persist to winter
Flowers: 5–8″   reddish-pink, beige with age   Early Oct.–
                                                      Persist into
                                                      winter

Foliage: green with white midvein   Texture: fine
Plant Form: upright-arching

Figure 11. Maiden Grass, Miscanthus sinensis *'Gracillimus,' derives its name from the curving, graceful flowers and foliage that are especially attractive in late fall and winter. An excellent plant for drying.*

This is the fine-textured, graceful variant of *Miscanthus sinensis*. It is a smaller plant, with long, very narrow curly leaves. The flowers also have curly branches which give them added interest for dried arrangements. Maiden Grass prefers the same location as *Miscanthus sinensis* and also forms dense clumps when placed in the landscape. The plants turn brown for the winter, but the flowers are of interest until early spring. Maiden Grass is suitable for use in the midground or background of a perennial border, as a specimen plant, a screen, or in water gardens (Figure 11).

The flowers are excellent for drying and dyeing.

Miscanthus sinensis "Variegatus"   Striped Eulalia Grass
    3–6′   Tender Perennial USDA Zone 5   Division
         Hardy Perennial USDA Zone 7
Flowers: 5–8″   pale pink, beige with age   Late Sept.–Oct.
Foliage: yellow, white, and green striped   Texture: medium
Plant Form: upright-open

This is one of the tallest variegated or striped grasses, but unfortunately this species is limited in use due to its tender winter hardiness. Because of its attractive foliage and flowers, Striped Eulalia Grass is suitable as a specimen plant, in the midground of a perennial border, in water gardens, or as a screen. Full sun is the ideal location and division is required every 5 to 7 years to keep the plants growing vigorously.

The flowers are ideal for dried arrangements however, in USDA Zone 5, they are often sparse and not as showy as the other variants of *Miscanthus sinensis*.

Miscanthus sinensis "Zebrinus"   Zebra Grass
    4–7′   Perennial, USDA Zone 5   Division
Flowers: 8–12″   pale yellow, beige   Mid-Sept.–Mid-Oct.
Foliage: green with horizontal yellow bands   Texture: medium
Plant Form: upright-narrow to upright-open

Zebra Grass has one of the most interesting foliage colors of all the ornamental grasses. The unique horizontal stripes make it ideal for a specimen plant, for a screen, an accent plant in the perennial border, or to add interest in water gardens (Figure 12).

It, just like the other members of the *Miscanthus* genus, requires a sunny location, for in shady sites the plants may require staking to keep them from falling over. The plants turn orange or brown with the first hard freeze in the fall, but the flowers are attractive if left on the plants through the winter.

The flowers are excellent for dried arrangements and for dyeing.

Figure 12. Zebra Grass, Miscanthus sinensis Zebrinus,' *has the largest flowers of the* Miscanthus sinensis *species. Propagation should only be done by division and any regular green shoots should be removed from a clump, as these can become more dominant as the plant matures.*

Figure 13. Basket Grass, Oplismenus compositus *'Vittatus,' can make an attractive interior plant if it is grown in high humidity, with lots of light and moist soil.*

Molinea caerulea "Variegata"   Purple Moor Grass
    1–2½'   Perennial, USDA Zone 5   Division
Flowers: 5–8"   yellow, green, purple   Late June–Late Aug.
Foliage: yellow-green striped   Texture: fine
Plant Form: upright-arching

This dainty short grass is grown for its attractive striped foliage and its graceful arching overall plant form. Purple Moor Grass is a distinctive addition to the landscape, as a specimen plant, in the foreground of a perennial border, in water gardens, as a ground cover, or as a rock garden specimen. The plants can also be grown indoors as potted plants. As a ground cover, a decorative mulch should be used between the plants.

A location of either full sun or partial shade is suitable, in moist but fertile soils. Moist, humid conditions around the plants may promote leaf spot diseases.

The flowers are attractive nearly all summer, but they are of little interest for use in dried arrangements.

Oplismenus compositus "Vittatus"   Basket Grass
    2–3' trailing stems   Indoor plant   Division, cuttings
Flowers: 1–2"   dark red, green   Sporadic
Foliage: green, white, pink, purple striped   Texture: medium
Plant Form: low, open and spreading

Basket Grass is one of the few grasses used solely as a potted plant. Its long trailing stems are covered with short, colorfully striped leaves. The flowers are not showy and may rarely be produced.

The plants grow rapidly and require repotting whenever the roots can be seen coming out of the bottom of the pot. Locations of full sun, constantly moist soil, and high humidity are best for large, colorful plants. A soil mix of one part peat, one part top soil, and one part sand, perlite, or vermiculite is quite satisfactory. During active growth, fertilize the plants every two weeks with a water-soluble fertilizer (20-20-20) or use a slow release fertilizer in the soil mix. Basket Grass is especially showy for hanging baskets (Figure 13).

Panicum virgatum   Switch Grass
   3–6′   Perennial, USDA Zone 5   Division, Seed
Flowers: 12–16″   dark red or purple, beige with age

Late July–Early Sept.

Foliage: green   Texture: medium
Plant Form: upright-narrow

Switch Grass is native to most of the United States. When grown as an ornamental, its merit lies in the upright-narrow plant form and the dense masses of wide-spreading flowers. Switch Grass is not a showy ornamental; it is best used in the water garden, as a screen, or in naturalized areas. It will grow in either full sun or partial shade in moist or dry soils. Although the plants turn brown in the winter, they remain upright and can form a valuable wildlife cover during the winter.

Switch Grass has a medium to bright yellow fall color in the Northeast. In light sandy soils, creeping rhizomes may cause the plants to spread slowly, but there are many varieties and cultivars of *Panicum virgatum* and not all of them have rhizomes. One variant, *Panicum virgatum* "Strictum," is shorter, 3 to 4 feeet tall, with smaller flowers that tend to bloom earlier than the species. *Panicum virgatum* "Rubrum" is also 3 to 4 feet tall and has leaves tinged with dark red.

Figure 14. Panicum virgatum, *Switch Grass, is native to North America and is a valuable plant for wildlife and conservation plantings.*

Pennisetum alopecuroides   Fountain Grass
  4–4½'   Perennial, USDA Zone 5   Division
Flowers: 6–8"   coppery-tan or reddish   Late Aug.–Early Oct.
Foliage: green   Texture: medium-fine
Plant Form: mound

This is truly one of the best grasses for use in landscaping. The medium-sized mound form is attractive and in late summer and through fall the plants are covered with coppery-tan flowers. In the northeast, Fountain Grass turns a yellow fall color as cooler weather sets in. During the winter the plants remain upright, but the flowers usually fall apart; thus there is little interest after late fall.

The plants are excellent for use in the perennial border, as a specimen plant, or in water gardens. Full sun or partial shade are suitable locations, but the plants should have room to develop their 3-to-4-foot mature diameter. Division is required every 5 to 10 years to prevent the center of the plant from dying (Figure 15).

The flowers, although quite attractive when borne on the plant, are seldom suitable for dried arrangements as they shatter readily with age.

Pennisetum setaceum   Crimson Fountain Grass
  2–3'   Hort. Annual, USDA Zone 5–8   Seed
       Perennial, USDA Zone 8–9
Flowers: 9–12"   dk. purple, red   Late July–Early Oct.
Foliage: green   Texture: fine
Plant Form: mound to upright-arching

Crimson Fountain Grass, often listed in the trade as *Pennisetum ruppellii*, is grown for its long, narrow purple flowers and the attractive mound which it forms at maturity. The plants are suitable for use in perennial or annual borders, in water gardens, or as specimen plants. Locations of full sun or very light shade produce the best plants. In warm climates, where Crimson Fountain Grass is a perennial, it often reseeds

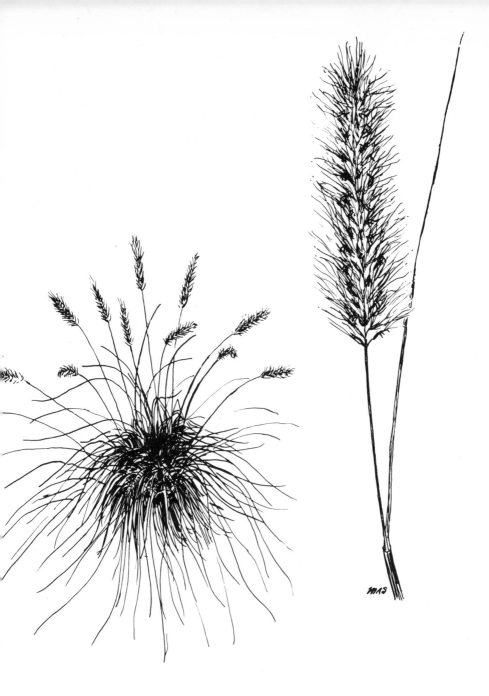

Figure 15. Fountain Grass, Pennisetum alopecuroides, *should be given a place in more gardens. If just one grass could be planted, this species would be a good selection.*

itself and may become a nuisance if the flowers are not picked before shattering. The plants turn beige for the winter and are of no value at this season, or in the fall after a hard frost.

The flowers shatter too easily to be used in dried arrangements, but their deep purple or red color is very decorative in fresh arrangements.

Pennisetum villosum   Feather Top
   1½–2½′   Hort. Annual, USDA Zone 5–8   Seed
           Perennial, USDA Zone 8 or 9
Flowers: 3–5″   tawny, white, light green   Late July–Late Sept.
Foliage: green   Texture: medium
Plant Form: mound to irregular

The overall form of this species of *Pennisetum* is not as desirable as the two just previously noted. Feather Top is grown chiefly for its white or ivory flowers ,which are quite numerous on each plant. Annual or perennial borders are the best garden location and full sun to light shade are preferable. The plants have no interest in fall or winter; after hard frosts the entire plant turns beige.

As with other species of *Pennisetum*, these flowers shatter easily when dry, but Feather Top is a lovely addition to fresh flower arrangements (Figure 17).

Phalaris arundinacea "Picta"   Ribbon Grass
   2–4½′   Perennial USDA Zone 4   Division
Flowers: 4–6″   white, pale pink   Early June–Mid-July
Foliage: white, green, pink striped   Texture: Medium
Plant Form: upright-open

Certainly one of the oldest decorative grasses is Ribbon Grass. The first herbals usually list this, for it has been grown for hundreds of years for its decorative, striped foliage. Unfortunately, there is one major drawback to using this plant—its creeping rhizomes are most invasive. To contain the plant, metal cans (with no bottoms) should be sunken into the ground

Figure 16. The feathery flowers of Pennisetum setaceum, *Crimson Fountain Grass, shown above, are slightly longer than* Pennisetum alopecuroides. *Crimson Fountain Grass is best used as a fresh cut flower, for the purple flower color fades if the spikes are dried.*

Figure 17. Feather Top, Pennisetum villosum, *has tawny or ivory flowers that are different and refreshing in fresh arrangements. The overall plants are irregular in form and not ideal garden specimens.*

around the plant roots, just after or prior to the initial planting.

When properly contained, the foliage of Ribbon Grass is a striking contrast in the perennial border, as a background for bright flowers, or as an accent in the spring and summer. The plants are quite tolerant of wet or poor soils, in either sun or partial shade. Heavy clay soils confine roots to some extent.

By late August, the lower leaves often turn brown and appear unattractive. The peak of showiness is in early spring through midsummer.

The flowers are of little interest for dried arrangements. The foliage can be used for variety and accent in fresh flower arrangements.

Phalaris canariensis   Canary Grass
    1–2′   Annual   Seed
Flowers: 1–2″   light green, beige   Mid-June–Mid-July
Foliage: green   Texture: medium
Plant Form: upright-open

Canary Grass is the commercial source of canary seed; the seeds are a favorite of many birds. These plants are grown only for their flowers, which are ideal for dried arrangements. The overall form is not attractive and a prominent place in the garden should not be planted with Canary Grass. After the flowers are produced, the plants rapidly turn brown. Locations of full sun with adequate moisture produce the best flowers. *Phalaris minor* is often sold in the trade as Canary Grass, the flowers are almost identical, except they are slightly smaller.

The dried flowers are somewhat difficult to dye, but well worth the effort.

Phleum pratense   Timothy
    1½–3′   Perennial, USDA Zone 4   Seed
Flowers: 2–5″   light green   Late June–Early Aug.
Foliage: green   Texture: medium
Plant Form: upright-narrow

The cultivated Timothy is an important grass for hay. It has escaped cultivation and can be found growing wild in fields and along roadsides throughout the U.S.

Although ornamental only for its dried flowers, Timothy could also be sown in a naturalized meadow or sunny field. The flowers are quite popular in florist shops and are almost always dyed bright colors. When first borne on the plant, the flowers often have a purple cast due to the numerous purple anthers.

Poa bulbosa   Bulbous Bluegrass
    8–24″   Perennial, USDA Zone 5   Division
Flowers: 2–4″   green, purple bulblets   Early June–Mid-June
Foliage: blue-green   Texture: fine
Plant Form: upright-arching

This is really more of a curiosity plant than a true ornamental. The flowers of Bulbous Bluegrass are proliferous—that is, instead of seeds being borne in the flower, there are small bulbets or plants borne in dense clusters. The weight of these plantlets makes the flowers nod and bend towards the ground. At maturity the plantlets fall off and if conditions are suitable, they begin to grow.

Although the flowers are borne quite early in the spring, they last only a short time and then, quite quickly, the entire plant dies. A site of full sun is required. The flowers have some interest in dried arrangements. The overall form of the plants is not desirable for landscaping.

Polypogon monspeliensis   Rabbit's-foot Grass
    5–18″   Annual   Seed
Flowers: 1–6″   light green   Mid-June–Late July
Foliage: green   Texture: medium
Plant Form: upright-narrow

This decorative annual turns into a mass of blooms by mid-July. In locations of full sun or very light shade, with fertile, well-drained soil, each plant will produce numerous flowers.

The overall appearance of Rabbit's-foot Grass is not particularly ornamental; the plants are usually grown just for the flowers. After flowering, the plants turn brown and die. Heavy winds and rain can knock the plants down; protected locations usually prevent this.

The flowers can be dyed or used in their natural color for arrangements. Often confused with Hare's-tail Grass, Rabbit's-foot Grass has a longer and narrower flower, and is usually light green rather than ivory or white.

Rhynchelytrum roseum   Ruby Grass
    2–4′   Hort. Annual, USDA Zone 5–9   Seed
              Perennial, USDA Zone 9
Flowers: 6–10″   ruby red fading to pink or silvery-white
Foliage: green, upper leaves   Late July–Early Oct.
        often tinged with purple   Texture: medium
Plant Form: upright-open to irregular

Ruby Grass, often listed in the trade as *Tricholaena rosea,* has been grown for years for its showy ruby red flowers (Figure 18). The plants themselves are irregular and very easily knocked over in winds and rain. In the annual or perennial border, Ruby Grass may be suitable if the location is in full sun. With fall frosts, the leaves turn brown and the plants have no interest.

In the southern U.S., especially in Florida, Ruby Grass has escaped cultivation and can be found along roadsides and in waste places.

The flowers are excellent for fresh arrangements; unfortunately, though, Ruby Grass does not retain its color in dried arrangements and the flowers often shatter with age.

Scirpus tabernaemontani "Zebrinus"   Striped Bullrush
    1½–3′   Perennial, USDA Zone 6   Division
Flowers: 1–2″   light green or yellow   Sporadic
Foliage: green and yellow striped   Texture: fine
Plant Form: upright-narrow

This is one of two grasses with foliage transversely banded green, yellow, and white. Striped Bullrush is one of the best grasses for water gardens; it will grow in water, at the edge of a pool, or in moist soil. The plants tolerate full sun but grow best in light to deep shade.

During the winter, the foliage remains semi-evergreen. The flowers, borne sporadically throughout the summer, are of little interest, and although they can be dried, they are small and not showy.

This is not a true grass; *Scirpus* is a member of the Sedge family.

Setaria italica   Foxtail Millet; Foxtail Grass
    2–3′   Annual   Seed
Flowers: 3–7″   yellow or green, gold with age   Mid-June–
                                                          Mid-July
Foliage: yellow-green   Texture: medium to coarse
Plant Form: upright-narrow

Foxtail Grass is often listed in the trade as an ornamental. Its decorative value, however, like so many other annuals, is

Figure 18. Ruby Grass, Rhynchelytrum roseum, *is truly a ruby red color. The flowers are best when used fresh; they fade with drying.*

restricted to its flowers, the overall plant form being unattractive in the garden. If used in the annual border, the plants can tolerate full sun or light shade, but their place is really only in the cut flower garden.

The flowers are dense when ripe with seed; often they nod and arch toward the ground at this stage. The small, shiny seeds usually fall out at maturity, but the flowers remain intact enough for dried arrangements. The flowers usually dye unevenly and their natural golden tan color at maturity is often preferable to the dyed colors.

Setaria palmifolia "Variegata"   Palm Grass
    2–4′   Indoor Plant except in Tropics   Division
Flowers: 8–12″   light green   Sporadic
Foliage: green, white, dk. purple striped   Texture: coarse
Plant Form: upright-open to irregular

Palm Grass may often be found in conservatories and older greenhouses as a large potted plant. Its long, arching leaves and upright-open form make it a good indoor plant. It is almost always grown indoors in the U.S., except possibly in the extreme southern part of the country. Indoors, it requires medium to high light intensity and fertile, well-drained soil with a high water-holding capacity.

The leaves of Palm Grass are interesting, for in addition to their being striped (usually near the margins) with yellow, white, and purple, they are plicate, or folded, as a fan.

The flowers, although often quite large, are not used in dried arrangements, because they are of little interest.

Sisyrinchium bellum   Blue-eyed Grass
    10–15″   Perennial, USDA Zone 6   Seed, Division
Flowers: 1″   pale blue, violet   Early July–Early Sept.
Foliage: green to blue-green   Texture: fine
Plant Form: irregular

Although Blue-eyed Grass is called a "grass" and is sold as an ornamental grass, it is really a member of the Iridaceae or

Iris family. Its leaves are grass-like, but the pale blue flowers have showy petals which give them away as not being true grasses.

This is a tender perennial which needs winter protection and grows best in full sun or light shade with moist soil. It can be planted in the rock garden, in water gardens, in naturalized areas, or in the foreground of a perennial border. In winter, the leaves turn a dark green or brown and have no interest.

When propagated from seed, flowers will be borne the first year, although they tend to be sporadic through late summer. The flowers can be used for fresh arrangements, though they are short-lived. They do not dry well for everlasting arrangements.

Sitanion hystrix   Squirrel's-tail Grass
    4–24″   Perennial, USDA Zone 4   Seed, Division
Flowers: 2–8″   beige   Mid-July–Late Aug.
Foliage: green   Texture: medium
Plant Form: upright-open

This perennial closely resembles *Hordeum jubatum* and *Hystrix patula*. It is grown primarily for the decorative flowers that have conspicuously long awns, or hair-like projections. The plants are suitable for use in the perennial border or in naturalized areas. The entire plant turns brown by early winter. Locations of full sun or light shade in dry or well-drained soils are suitable.

Squirrel's-tail Grass has very attractive flowers for use in dried arrangements. However, they must be picked early, just as they emerge from the leaves, or the flowers will shatter when dry.

Sorghastrum nutans   Indian Grass
    3–5′   Perennial, USDA Zone 5   Seed, Division
Flowers: 12–15″   golden brown   Mid-Aug.–Mid-Sept.
Foliage: green   Texture: medium
Plant Form: upright-open

Indian Grass has long been a native plant in the midwestern U.S. It is especially useful for planting in naturalized areas, or perhaps in an informal perennial border. The overall plant form is fairly attractive, and the flowers are quite showy when borne in late summer. Grow in full sun, in a wide variety of soil types.

In the Northeast, Indian Grass turns an orange or purple fall color, and the plants remain upright with little interest in the winter.

The flowers are a shiny brown with bright yellow anthers (male flower parts) when in full flower. As they age the color turns to a deep brown; they are suitable for dried arrangements.

Spartina pectinata "Aureo-marginata"   Cord Grass
    4–8′   Perennial, USDA Zone 5   Division
Flowers: 6–15″   light yellow, beige   Late Aug.–Late Sept.
Foliage: shiny green with yellow   Texture: medium to coarse
        marginal stripes
Plant Form: upright-open to upright-arching

Cord Grass, long known in the trade as *Spartina michauxiana* "Aureo-marginata," is one of the best grasses for moist or wet soils near either fresh or salt water. It is native to sandy soils and with its vigorous creeping rhizomes, the plants will often overcome a large area in light soils. This is advantageous for sand binding, but not in a small garden area. Locations of full sun or light shade are ideal. Cord Grass has a bright yellow fall color which is showy in October, after which the plants turn beige and have little winter interest. Suitable for the perennial border, as a specimen plant, in water gardens, or naturalized areas (Figure 19).

The flowers are attractive and suitable for arrangements; however, they are not one of the best for dyeing.

Figure 19. Spartina pectinata 'Aureo-marginata,' Cord Grass, is a good sand binder near fresh or salt water. Plant this in a container in the garden to keep it in place.

Stenotaphrum secundatum "Variegatum"   Striped St. Augustine
Grass
3–12″   Perennial, USDA Zone 7   Division
Flowers: 2–5″   light green   Mid-July–Late Aug.
Foliage: green and white striped   Texture: medium to coarse
Plant Form: low, open, and spreading

The only variegated or striped form of a turf grass is Striped St. Augustine Grass. Because of its vigorous stoloniferous rooting habit, this is an ideal ground cover plant. It can be mowed and treated as a turfgrass. Burle Marx, a landscape architect in South America, has used large square blocks of Striped St. Augustine Grass with regular green St. Augustine Grass to form a giant living checkerboard pattern in his designs in South America.

This is a warm-season or tropical grass; it is grown in the North only as a potted conservatory plant. Outdoors, locations of full sun in fertile, well-drained soils are best. Indoors, the plants require high light intensity and should be cut back frequently to keep the creeping stems in check.

The flowers are not showy and do not merit use in dried arrangements.

Stipa pennata   Feather Grass
2–3′   Perennial, USDA Zone 5   Seed, Division
Flowers: 10–14″   beige, light green   Early July–Early August
Foliage: green   Texture: medium
Plant Form: upright-open

This is one of the most decorative grasses grown primarily for its flowers, which are long, slender, feathery panicles borne in midsummer. The plants can be grown in perennial borders in sun or light shade, as specimen plants, or near water gardens. Fertile, well-drained soils are ideal. The plants have no winter interest.

The seeds of *Stipa* may be quite difficult to germinate; it is best to buy plants if available. Each flower that later becomes a seed of Feather Grass is 10 to 14 inches long. The seed itself is only about ½ inch long, but the long, feathery awn that projects from the seed is the most conspicuous part. The long awn is sensitive to air moisture and twists and turns as the humidity changes. For this reason Feather Grass and other *Stipa* sp. are often injurious to animals if these seeds become lodged in their hair.

The seeds often become brittle and fall from the awn at maturity, but the long, feathery awns stay intact for use in arrangements.

Dyed and natural colors often are available from florists. John Parkinson, one of the first authors of horticulture books, writes of this grass in 1656 as being one of the loveliest grasses; its plumes were used "for feathers in beds and for decoration on lady's hats."

Several other species of *Stipa* are decorative. *Stipa arundinacea* is a 2½-to-3-foot mound with reddish-orange foliage. *Stipa capillata*, Spear Grass, is a perennial with smaller (3-to-6-inch) awns. *Stipa elegantissima* grows 2 to 3 feet tall and has a panicle which is half the height of the plant; the flowers are sometimes purple-tinged; the grass is a perennial native to Australia. *Stipa gigantea* is a 7-foot-tall perennial; the showy yellow panicles are 10 to 15 inches long and borne in mid-July.

Triticum sp.   Wheat
    2–3½'   Annuals   Seed
Flowers: 2–5"   light green, beige   Mid-July–Late Aug.
Foliage: green   Texture: medium
Plant Form: upright-narrow

Many species of the cultivated form of wheat are grown for their use in dried arrangements. These plants have no decorative value for landscaping and their only use is for cut, dried flowers. *Triticum spelt*, Spelt, is sold in the trade as an ornamental grass; it does not have the long awns that other species have. Many of the varieties of *Triticum aestivum* have long awns or hair-like projections.

The dried flowers are often dyed bright colors; they require a longer time in dye solutions than most other grasses.

Barley and wheat are quite similar in appearance; the difference between these two grasses is explained under *Hordeum vulgare*, Barley.

Uniola latifolia	Northern Sea Oats, Spangle Grass	
3–5'	Perennial, USDA Zone 5	Division, Seed
Flowers: 10–12"	dk. green to reddish-brown bronze in winter	Late July– Persist into winter

Foliage: green   Texture: medium
Plant Form: upright-narrow to upright-arching

Northern Sea Oats is one of the best grasses for any garden. Its only limitation is that it will grow taller and be a darker green color in full or partial shade. It is an asset to shady, naturalized areas, water gardens, perennial borders, and makes an ideal specimen plant. There are three seasons of interest in Northern Sea Oats: summer when it is in flower, fall when the foliage turns a rich bronze, and winter when the flowers persist on the plant and it remains an attractive, upright-arching specimen. It is one of the few grasses that grows best in shady areas. Fertile, well-drained soils are ideal.

In growing plants from seed, germination is often poor. This is because many of the flowers within each small spikelet are sterile and produce no seed.

The flowers are excellent for dried arrangements; even if picked when mature, they rarely shatter. This is one of the most difficult grasses to dye, however, because the flowers should be bleached to remove their color before dyeing. Bleaching, either by sun or liquid chlorine chemicals, is a difficult process. The flowers are quite attractive in their natural color (Figure 20).

Figure 20. The counterpart of Sea Oats is Spangle Grass, Northern Sea Oats, Uniola latifolia, *an attractive addition to any border.*

Uniola paniculata   Sea Oats
   3–6'   Perennial, USDA Zone 7   Division
Flowers: 8–16"   light green, beige   Late July–Persist into
                                            winter
Foliage: green   Texture: fine
Plant Form: upright-narrow to upright-arching

Sea Oats is native to the sand dunes of the seacoast from Virginia south to Florida and west to Texas and eastern Mexico. It is also reported to be found on Long Island, N.Y., and perhaps as far north as Cape Cod, Mass. In most areas, the plants are protected by law for their extensively creeping rhizomes which are invaluable sand binders.

Because of these invasive rhizomes, Sea Oats does not have a place in formal perennial gardens. It is best suited for water gardens and sand dunes in locations of full sun. Plants of Sea Oats are rarely available in the trade, and as stated earlier, law prohibits their removal from natural coastal areas. The seeds are, in many cases, sterile so the plants cannot be propagated from seed.

Property owners along the coastal areas who are interested in obtaining Sea Oats (or other beach grasses) for planting should first contact their nearest Sea Grant office for information. The nearest Sea Grant office can be obtained by writing to the land grant College of Agriculture for each coastal state. Sea Grant officials can advise property owners as to the best methods of conservation plants along sand dunes and beaches.

The flowers of Sea Oats are one of the most popular for dried arrangements and they are readily available from florist or specialty shops. Sea Oats is easier to dye than Northern Sea Oats because the flowers are naturally a lighter beige, and thus bleaching previous to dyeing is not as essential.

Zea mays var. *japonica*   Ornamental Corn
   2½–4'   Annual   Seed
Flowers: 4–7"   beige   Early Aug.–Mid-Sept.
Foliage: white, yellow, pink, purple, and green striped
Plant Form: upright-narrow   Texture: coarse

Ornamental Corn is a dwarf form of regular corn, grown for its colorful striped foliage. The plants should be grown in full sun with fertile soil. Regardless of where this plant is placed in the garden, it usually becomes a specimen plant or focal point because of its coarse foliage and bright color. It can be located in perennial borders, in water gardens, or, of course, as a specimen plant.

The lower leaves usually turn brown and become unattractive by late summer.

The flowers are of little or no value for dried arrangements.

This plant is sometimes listed in the trade as *Zea mays* "Versicolor," *Zea mays* "Variegata," and *Zea mays* "Quadricolor."

Zizania aquatica   Wildrice
   6–9′   Annual   Seed
Flowers: 12–20″   light green   Late July–Late Sept.
Foliage: green   Texture: medium
Plant Form: upright-open

Wildrice is native to nearly all of the eastern and midwestern United States. It is often found in ponds, along ditches, or wherever moist or wet soil is abundant. It is a valuable plant for water gardens, for it will grow in shallow standing water as well as wet soils. Sun or light shade are ideal locations.

The flowers are attractive for arrangements; however they often shatter with age.

Wildrice was used to a limited extent by northern tribes of Indians for food. It is an important food source and shelter for wildlife and waterfowl, and is often planted for this purpose on game preserves.

Appendix

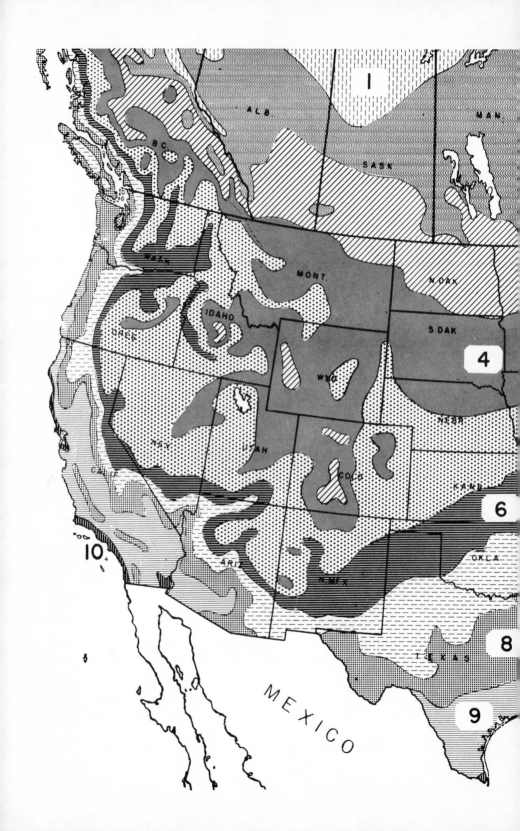

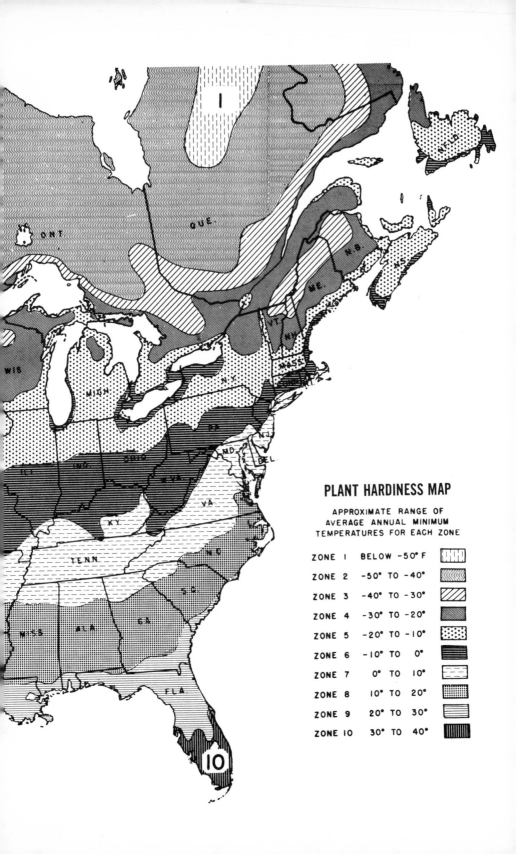

PLANT HARDINESS MAP

APPROXIMATE RANGE OF
AVERAGE ANNUAL MINIMUM
TEMPERATURES FOR EACH ZONE

ZONE 1   BELOW −50° F
ZONE 2   −50° TO −40°
ZONE 3   −40° TO −30°
ZONE 4   −30° TO −20°
ZONE 5   −20° TO −10°
ZONE 6   −10° TO   0°
ZONE 7   0° TO 10°
ZONE 8   10° TO 20°
ZONE 9   20° TO 30°
ZONE 10   30° TO 40°

Glossary

ANNUAL—completing one life cycle from seed to flowering in one growing season and then dying; usually propagated from seed.

AWN—slender hair-like projection(s) arising from the small flowers of grasses; variable in length and texture.

BASAL—pertaining to the base of the plant, at ground level; arising from or occurring at the base.

BRISTLE—slender hair-like projections arising from the petiole or branches of the inflorescence, sometimes surrounding the spikelet.

CORMS—very short, thick, firm fleshy stems, usually broader than high, just below the ground or at ground level.

CESPITOSE—forming tufts or mounds of foliage.

FIBROUS ROOTS—a root system in which the roots are finely divided, usually in a clump.

GLAUCOUS—covered with a bluish or whitish substance which rubs off.

HORTICULTURAL ANNUAL—plants are treated as annuals in cold climates, but as perennials in warmer regions.

INFLORESCENCE—the total flowering structure and arrangement of flowers on the main stem.

LIGULE—the small membrane or ring of hairs that occurs on the upper side of the leaves, just at the junction of the leaf blade and the sheath that wraps around the stem; reduced or absent in some species.

PANICLE—an open, often branched and spreading flowering structure; one type of inflorescence.

PERENNIAL—a plant which lives for an indefinite number of growing seasons; usually propagated from division, perhaps seed; may or may not flower the first growing season, but continues to grow and flower thereafter.

RHIZOMES—underground stems (resembling roots) usually growing horizontally and rooting at the nodes.

RHIZOMATOUS—with rhizomes.

SPIKE—a narrow and usually longer than wide inflorescence, the flowers borne along one main stem.

SPIKELET—the small flowering unit of grasses, consisting of a series of bracts placed one inside another, attached to a branch or the main flowering stem; there are many spikelets in one inflorescence.

STOLONS—horizontal stems, usually prostrate or trailing at ground level, always above the ground, often rooting at the nodes.

STOLONIFEROUS—with stolons.

Sources of Ornamental Grasses

The following list has been compiled for assistance in purchasing ornamental grasses. No discrimination is intended to nurseries not included in this listing.

Retail Nurseries, Ornamental Grass Plants

Henry Field Seed and Nursery Company
407 Sycamore Street
Shenandoah, Iowa 51602

Hillier and Sons Nursery
Jermyns Lane
Winchester, Hampshire
England

McNicols Landscaping
RD #1, Box 33
Nassau Commons
Lewes, Delaware 19959
(*Ammophilia arenaria* "Cape")

Martin Viette Nurseries
Route 25A
East Norwich, New York 11732
(does not ship plants)

Palette Gardens
26 W. Zion Hill Rd.
Quakertown, Pa. 18951
50¢ for catalog

Perry's Hardy Plant Farm
Enfield, Middlesex
England

Wayside Gardens Company
Mentor Avenue
Mentor, Ohio 44060

The Wild Garden
Box 487
Bothell, Washington 98011
($1.00 for catalog)

Retail Seedsmen, Ornamental Grass Seed

De Giorgi Co. Inc.
1409 Third Street
Council Bluffs, Iowa 51501

George W. Park Seed Co., Inc.
Greenwood, South Carolina 29647

Clyde Robin Seed Co., Inc.
P.O. Box 2855
Castro Valley, California 94546

Stokes Seeds, Inc.
Box 548
Buffalo, New York 14240

Thompson and Morgan, Ltd.
P.O. Box 24
401 Kennedy Blvd.
Somerdale, New Jersey 08083

Wholesale Nurseries, Ornamental Grass Plants

Bluemount Nurseries, Inc.
2103 Blue Mount Road
Monkton, Maryland 21111

Kurt Bluemel, Inc.
2543 Hess Rd.
Fallston, Md. 21047

Monrovia Nursery Company
P. O. Box Q
18331 East Foothill Blvd.
Azusa, California 91702

Select Nursery, Inc.
12831 East Central Avenue
Brea, California 92621

Index

° Names listed in parentheses are synonyms. They are not recognized as the correct name according to the most recent literature by the L. H. Bailey Hortorium staff at Cornell University, the *Manual of Cultivated Plants* by L. H. Bailey (Macmillan, 1949) and *Manual of the Grasses of the United States*, A. S. Hitchcock (Govt. Printing Office, Washington, D. C., 1950).